TRUE STORIES.

it
happened
to me

To the girls who shared their stories.
Thanks for your trust and honesty.

To Mum, Dad and Simon.

All names and locations have been changed.
All photographs are posed by models.

First published 1996 by
Macmillan Children's Books
a division of Macmillan Publishers Limited
25 Eccleston Place, London SW1W 9NF
and Basingstoke

Associated companies throughout the world

ISBN 0 330 34703 9

Copyright © Lesley Johnston and MIZZ Magazine 1996

The right of Lesley Johnston and MIZZ Magazine to be identified as
the authors of this book has been asserted by them in accordance
with the Copyright, Designs and Patents Act 1988.

1 3 5 7 9 8 6 4 2

A CIP catalogue record for this book is available from the British Library.

Printed by Mackays of Chatham plc, Chatham, Kent.

MIZZ
True life stories

it
happened
to me

Lesley Johnston

MACMILLAN

Contents

"I TRACED MY REAL MOTHER, AND SHE DIDN'T WANT TO KNOW"

Photograph posed by model

"I'd introduce myself to people by saying, 'I'm Marianne and I'm adopted'"

Marianne, 18 has always known she was adopted and didn't feel curious about her natural parents until last year. Then she wished she had never started her search because her real mother was not happy to be traced...

Even when I was tiny, I knew I was adopted and always thought of myself as special because Mum and Dad told me I had been chosen out of all the other babies. I had a happy home life, loved my parents and was proud of being different to other kids. I'd introduce myself to people by saying, 'I'm Marianne

and I'm adopted' so I never had a problem with telling other people.

Mum and Dad had told me that my real mum had kept me for six weeks before she had given me up to a Catholic adoption agency. Staff told my parents she'd come down from Scotland after being 'used and abused' by my natural father and thrown out by her family. I even had a document from them with her signature on it, 'M. Brown', and it also mentioned my 'real' name, Fiona. I didn't want to know any more than that because I was happy to go on without the details. Why cause trouble when I got on so well with the parents who loved and looked after me?

> "I wondered if my real mother was out there, thinking about me too"

> "I realized I was going to have to trace her or I would never know myself properly"

But then suddenly on my sixteenth birthday I made the decision to look for her. I wondered if my natural mother was out there somewhere, thinking about me too. Maybe it was because I'd just gone for my first job and had to give them details of my family's medical history. There could have been heart disease or even mental illness in my background and I wouldn't know. I decided I was going to have to trace her or I'd never know myself properly.

I went into the registrar's in Liverpool without a clue about what I was looking for, but I knew I'd been born in the city so that's where I should start. I lied (sort of) and told the girl at the front desk that I was Fiona Brown and I wanted to see my birth certificate.

She must have been new, because instead of telling me I needed to have permission from social services or that I was too young, she handed the certificate over. The search had begun.

The document gave me all sorts of new information, and for the first time I knew what the 'M' in M. Brown stood for. It was Martine. But I couldn't put a name to my dad; it said 'father unknown' instead.

At the time of my birth, Martine was a nurse and she'd given what sounded like the name of a hospital in Aberdeen as her address. So as soon as I got out of the registrar's I decided I would make some phone calls.

Directory enquiries told me there was no listing for that name, so I thought maybe the hospital had closed down years ago, and decided to call round some others. I eventually discovered that the name was actually of an old family house on the outskirts of the town. I couldn't believe it. I knew where Martine lived – or at least where she'd been living. I was getting closer!

My next move was to call the parish priest for that area as I thought Martine might have been known to him; but he didn't want to get involved. He said that if my mother was who he thought she was, then I'd better not come to look for her. Her family all looked very distinctive and alike, so if I looked like them too I would only have to set foot in their tiny village for people to notice me. He asked if I was very tall and blonde, with fair skin. I knew he could be right – he'd described my looks perfectly.

"I felt as though I needed some support, so I rang social services"

For almost two years I was too scared to continue because I didn't want to cause trouble, or to hurt my adoptive parents. I did feel I needed some support, though, so I rang my local social services who said that now I was 18, they could assign me someone to help.

My social worker, Anne, said I could have a look at the files from the adoption agency, and showed me a folder with my whole official history in it. I was apprehensive as I looked through the documents, but they didn't tell me anything I hadn't known already.

There was an address for the house I'd searched for though, and Anne asked if I wanted her to try to contact Martine if she could and perhaps set up a meeting. I agreed, but tried not to get my hopes up. Three weeks went by and then Anne phoned me to say Martine had called her. I was so shocked – suddenly this woman I'd never thought of as a real person was reality. She was making phone calls and talking about me. I felt panicky and excited. What had she said? Would she see me? Anne told me the whole story ...

"Martine hadn't told anyone she was pregnant and had worn a corset to try and disguise her bump"

Martine hadn't told a soul she was pregnant. She'd worn a corset to try to hide her bump until she got to Liverpool where she didn't know anyone who would recognize her. She'd told her parents she was moving there to find work. My father had been desperate to marry her, but she didn't want to know him; and the part that hurt for me was that he'd told her he wanted to keep me and take me back to Ireland, where he was from. It made me so angry. How could she have made those decisions? I'd always automatically assumed my real father hadn't loved me, but he had and didn't get the chance to raise me.

Martine had gone to a convent for advice, and when it was arranged for the adoption agency to meet her she was so scared they wouldn't help that she'd told the sorry tale of abuse I'd always thought was true. I was bitterly disappointed that I'd believed her lies.

Anne paused before she explained that Martine had refused to meet me. She had a husband now and another daughter, and neither of them knew that she'd had a baby before. Anne got the impression Martine was scared of her husband and was desperate to ensure he didn't find out. I felt sorry for her then. What sort of life was that, to have to lie about your past and keep things from the people you loved? It was nothing like the relationship I had with my parents. Somehow, I felt better then, realizing what I had at home.

I told my parents everything when they came home from work. Mum had tears in her eyes, but they were brilliant about it. For all three of us, it was like laying the 'ghost' of my natural mother to rest. We could get on with our lives, now I'd found Martine.

From then on we've got on so well and I've felt really settled again. I keep in touch with Anne, although I know the search is over for now. I've sometimes thought I could write to Martine, but I can't risk her family knowing. Anyway, now I know the truth about my history I feel like I can forget all about it again. I'm just happy being me, and from now on my sights are set on the future rather than the past.

Should you look for your natural parents?

If you are adopted, it's very likely that you'll want to search for your natural parents, but you may want to ask yourself some questions first before looking. Check the following statements. Can you agree with all of them?

☐ I haven't rushed into the decision to look for my real parents. It's something I have thought about for a long time.

☐ I understand that I might not be successful in my search.

☐ I realize that searching for my biological mother and father might alter my relationship with my adoptive parents.

☐ I've asked for help in my search either from social services, or from an agency such as NORCAP.

☐ I realize my natural mother may now have other children who have not been adopted.

☐ I will be prepared for the possibility that my natural mother may not want to see me.

☐ I am over 18 and therefore legally entitled to start my search.

☐ I realize not all my friends or adoptive family will support my search.

If you have not been able to tick every statement here, you may not be fully prepared to begin the search for your biological parents. Talk to your social worker, adoptive parents or an organization like NORCAP. They should be able to help sort out the emotional and practical problems that are all too common when adopted children set out to explore their backgrounds.

Advice

Think you are adopted?

You may suspect you are adopted even though your parents have never mentioned anything about it. The only way to find out for sure is to ask, but think carefully before you confront your parents. As you grow up it can be quite natural to feel very different to the rest of your family, to feel like you don't have anything in common with brothers, sisters or parents. But that doesn't mean that you are adopted; after all we are all individuals. If you think that asking your parents might upset them, then confide in a close relative or family friend before you go any further.

Do you want to find your real parents?

If you are under 18 there is not a lot you can do other than ask adoptive relatives about your background and hope they have some leads. Above that age you are legally entitled to look at a copy of your birth certificate at the relevant records office. This should give details of your birth mother, but may simply read 'father unknown' rather than name him (this would have been your mother's choice when your birth was registered). Please remember that it's best to talk to someone about your feelings before you start looking, because successful or not, the search for your parents could affect you deeply.

Who can help?

Your social services should be able to help – look in the phone book for details of your local office. NOR-CAP (The National Council for Counselling Adoptees and Parents) offer a counselling service to help you talk about your fears before looking for your biological parents. They can put you in contact with other adopted children and with parents who have had their child adopted, and this might help you to talk about your real feelings before going any further.

NORCAP also provide an excellent intermediary service, which means they will help make enquiries about your natural mother on your behalf and perhaps pave the way for a reunion if both parties think this is acceptable.

There may be problems

You may not realize the full implications of finding your natural mother, as it can cause a lot of emotional upset and trauma on both sides. Not only could a reunion change your life, it could also affect your natural parents' relationships with their partners and other children they may have had since giving you up. They may not have told their current partner or family of the fact that they once gave a child up for adoption, so they might not want to know you when you do try to get in contact. And if they do welcome the chance to meet, how will you feel if you don't get on?

What about your adoptive parents?

Although they may have prepared themselves for the possibility of it happening one day, your adoptive parents may be hurt or even jealous when you feel the need to search for your natural family. NORCAP also offer a service to them, to help them understand that your need to search for your natural parents doesn't mean that your feelings for your adoptive family have changed. Finding your background is more about finding the real you.

Marianne's advice

Tracing your real parents is so worthwhile, no matter what your reasons, but you do have to prepare yourself for a big disappointment if they don't want to know. You also have to pave the way with your adoptive parents and friends too. I couldn't expect people to help in my search. Some of my friends said they felt I was being disloyal to my adoptive parents and so disapproved of what I was doing. That meant I needed Anne, my social worker, more than ever, and it was so brilliant to have someone there who was specially trained to listen and to help me look. This isn't the sort of thing you should handle on your own and I would tell anyone even thinking about looking into their background to enlist the help of experts. There's loads of help out there if you ask for it.

Contacts

NORCAP (National Council For Counselling Adoptees and Parents)
112 Church Road, Wheatley, Oxfordshire OX33 1LU

BAAF (British Agencies For Adoption and Fostering)
Skyline House, 200 Union Street, London SE1 0LX

Post-Adoption Centres
5 Torriano Mews, Torriano Avenue, London NW5 2RZ

Advice line: 0171 284 0555 (open from 10.30 a.m. to 1.30 p.m. on Mondays, Tuesdays, Wednesdays and Fridays; and from 5.30 p.m. to 7.30 p.m. on Thursdays)

When writing to any of the above, please don't forget to enclose a stamped addressed envelope.

"MY HOT DATE WAS A DISASTER!"

Photograph posed by model

"I hope I ruin his reputation for ever"

When 15-year-old Lilly was asked out by a boy she'd fancied for years, she knew it was going to be the most memorable night of her life. It certainly was, but for all the wrong reasons …

Matt was a boy I knew vaguely, and had always liked. He was a bit of a troublemaker at times and had got suspended from school once, but he was like a sex symbol and everyone fancied him. He happened to be the best-looking boy in our area and could easily have been a model. I certainly never thought that I could have been in with a chance with him, and when he went to a different senior school to me I thought I'd seen the last of him.

"I couldn't believe it – he liked me!"

I went out to the pictures with my brothers one night, and while we were sitting waiting for the film to start I heard someone calling me and it was Matt and his friend, a few rows behind us. I felt a bit nervous even talking to him – I only had to look at him and I got embarrassed. He was gorgeous! When we came out of the cinema he had waited to see me and was giving me a lot of really flattering compliments and said we should go out some time. I couldn't believe it – he liked me!

I thought about Matt a lot over the next few days and when I got back from walking the dog the next Saturday morning my mum told me a boy had been on the phone for me. I guessed it was Matt, so I rang him back, which took a lot of courage because I could have been wrong! But I wasn't and he was really sweet and chatted for ages. He said there was a party on that night that he wanted to take me to, so he'd meet me at the same cinema at eight and we'd go on from there.

My friend Caitlin spent the afternoon helping me get ready, so by the time I left to go and meet Matt I was wearing all her best clothes.

"The first warning sign came before we'd even spoken"

I waited for Matt, and the first warning sign that things were going to go wrong came before we'd even spoken. As I was watching him walk over the road he fell over. I was really laughing but when he came over and pecked me on the cheek I realized he was dead drunk. I was a bit annoyed but at least I didn't have to be as awkward and nervous with him. He would hardly have noticed.

When we got to the bus stop he sat down, pulled me on to his knee and started snogging me like we had been going out for ages. Part of me was really turned on but I was also thinking, 'Wait a minute!' But at this stage I still thought the situation was funny, even when we got on the bus and I had to pay his fare.

> "I was sure he'd be all right when we got to the party, but he was even worse"

I think at the time I fancied him so much I didn't say anything. Even when he made faces at the lady next to us, I almost wanted to laugh because he was so mad. But when it was our stop he put his face right up to hers and said 'nosy old bitch' just because she'd looked over. I thought he'd gone too far. I had a go at him and he started messing around trying to kiss me and saying it was just his idea of a laugh. I was sure he'd be all right when we got to the party, but things got even worse ...

I got dumped in the kitchen and Matt walked off somewhere. I didn't know anyone so I went to look for him and soon knew why he'd disappeared. In the other room I saw him leaning over a table snorting what I thought was cocaine. I asked if that's what it was and they all laughed at me. Alan told me it was whizz and I should have a bit because it was going to be an all-night party and I might need the energy if he knew Matt! They all laughed like I was some tart.

I felt really sick and frightened because none of my mates were into drugs. Matt asked if I wanted some of the speed and he was a total mess. He was out of his tree! I kept asking him where he had put my coat because I wanted to go home, but he pushed me aside and started walking off again. Instead of being scared I suddenly got angry. I said, 'Where the hell do you think you're going?' and grabbed his arm, but he spun round and lashed out with his other arm and caught me in the eye. It was really painful and I was in tears but people were too unconcerned or too out of it to help. Matt went off like nothing had happened, even though I was bleeding. I couldn't believe it, I just wanted to get out.

I ran out of the house, not even really knowing where I was, and I saw a taxi after half an hour's walk. I was freezing because my jacket, or rather Caitlin's, was back there. Of course I had no money either because that was in the pocket, but the driver was really nice and said I could get it when I got home.

> "Mum was screaming and asking if she should ring the police"

I fell in the door in a right state and my dad was panicking because I had blood all down my face where Matt's ring had cut me. Mum was so shocked and asking if she should ring the police, but I persuaded her not to.

They made me tell them everything, but I left out the drugs bit because my dad would have gone mental. I also refused to say who I'd been out on my date with because I also know Dad would have found him eventually and got him done for assault.

I thought they were going to hit the roof. I was grounded for two months because I wouldn't tell them where I'd been, even though what happened wasn't my fault. My mum said she'd be keeping a close eye on me and she wouldn't trust me again, but the worst thing about it all is that I feel like I can't trust anyone else. Everyone else can go out with boys and have a great time, but I had a complete disaster and it will take me a while to get over it.

Matt phoned me the next morning – luckily for him I answered. He didn't even apologize: he said he was ringing to say I had made a fool of him and he never wanted to see me again. I didn't get the chance to say what I thought because he put the phone down. I never want to speak to him again, but I did try to speak to Alan, the bloke who had the party, because I wanted to get Caitlin's jacket back. He said Matt had it, so I've had to buy a new one for her.

I know so many girls who would die for a night with Matt, and I've done my best to tell them what a total nightmare he is. I hope I ruin his reputation for ever. I've only seen him once since then and that was awful – he stared at me but I ignored him. His new girlfriend goes to my school and has been slagging me off and saying I'm jealous, but I've never been so glad to walk away from someone in my life. He's awful and she'll find that out soon. As far as I'm concerned, she's welcome to him.

Could you have a disastrous date?

Look at the following ten points. Note down whether you agree or disagree with the statements, and we'll tell you how to score afterwards …

- I wouldn't ever think about going out with a lad I didn't fancy immediately. It's unlikely my feelings would change for him.
- I sometimes find it quite difficult to talk to boys like I would chat to one of my female friends.
- If he's the one who has asked me out on the date then I expect him to pay for everything.
- It's better if we go out somewhere my mates are going to be so I can escape with them if I hate him.
- Snogging's one thing, but it's difficult to say anything on a first date if he goes a bit further than I would like him to.
- If he didn't make me fall for him in the first half hour then I'd probably go off him for good.
- It's not cool to be too enthusiastic if he suggests another date – even if the first one went really well.
- If my parents weren't happy about me going out on the date, I'd lie and say I was going somewhere else.
- No matter how much I fancy a boy I find it difficult to let him know it!
- It's a good idea to try to have a drink before you meet your date; that way you'll find it easier to get on with him.

Scoring

Give yourself one point for every time you agreed. Give yourself two points for every time you disagreed. If you scored ...

18 or more points

First dates don't phase you and because you go in there not expecting any romantic thunderbolts to strike, you might just get a pleasant surprise! You find it easy to relax and enjoy yourself, so you can have a good time getting to know him. You know you fancy him, so now you've got plenty of time to find out all the other important stuff.

Tip: Don't put on a show, no matter how much you like him. Your biggest asset is making lads feel just like they're talking to a mate.

Ideal date location: McDonald's, your house or anywhere you can just sit together and talk!

15–18 points

OK, so you don't always choose the right boy to go out with, or to fancy in the first place, but you have to give him a chance first to be able to reject him later! You may feel despondent, but give it time and you will find the right one for you. To be in with a better chance, make sure your dates are organized to perfection. Now all you have to worry about is whether the two of you actually get on or not.

Tip: Do a bit of sneaky research on him first and find out more about what makes him tick. Nerves go out the window when you've made a mental list of things to talk about.

Ideal date location: Bowling, skating or swimming if you feel comfortable in your cossie! You've got things to do if you feel awkward, but plenty of chances to get to know him too.

10–14 points

You might be on the way to a night to remember – for the wrong reasons. Think more carefully next time about where you go – and who you go with! You've probably had a few disasters in your time because you feel so flattered when a boy shows a vague interest in you that you don't stop to think whether you actually like him or not. And if you go on the date and realize you've made the wrong decision it's likely you'll freeze him out until he gets the message!

Tip: If you get asked out, say you want a little bit of time to decide. Don't take the mick and get back to him in a fortnight, but decide if this is right for you before jumping into saying yes.

Ideal date location: A walk to the cinema, a movie, and then the walk back home again. You'll have a while to suss him out, a whole movie to make your mind up about him, and a journey home to snog him if you like him!

Advice

How to have the perfect date

You might not have chosen the perfect partner, but how are you meant to know that, unless you've at least tried going out on a date with the boy in question? Here's how to make sure you don't end up experiencing the worst moments of your life on that difficult first date ...

Be yourself
What happens if this does turn into a more long-term relationship? If you try to be something you're not on the night in question then you're going to have to pro-long the fantasy for even longer if he wants to see you again! So don't try telling any lies about you, your family, or what you get up to in your spare time. You'll only get found out later and feel really embarrassed about it!

Talk to him like a mate
It's easy to get nervous, but if you clam up and decide

you're going to let him be the one to do all the talking then you might end up with a very short-lived friendship that could have turned into a beautiful romance! Pretend you don't go wobbly when you see him and he's just like your spotty cousin. Talk about anything you like, but be chatty.

Don't be scared of a snog!

It's totally up to you if you want to kiss on the first date, because nothing's compulsory. If he does try to make a move on you, don't be scared – if you don't feel comfortable getting to grips with a kiss just yet then just tell him; it's no big deal. Every couple snogs differently, so there's no point in us trying to tell you what's right for you and your new boyfriend. Just try to remember that the secret to a good kiss is relaxation. Follow what his mouth does, try out anything you like the feel of and enjoy yourself.

Say no if you want to!

On a first date you shouldn't be expected to do anything that makes you feel uncomfortable, and that includes the physical stuff too. It can be difficult to relax when you don't know what's 'expected' of you. But that's just the point – it's up to you too to decide how far things go and you don't 'owe' him anything. So, if things get a bit too heated for your liking then don't hold back – say exactly how you feel.

Make it a private date

Double dates can work for that all-important first meeting, but there will come a time when the two of you are going to have to be all on your own. That's when you don't need mates in the row behind you at the pictures or the next table at McDonald's. If you get him all alone you can be yourselves, without keeping up appearances or running the risk of your pals slagging you off later for being lovey-dovey. Keep the date for just you and him but take Lilly's advice (below) and make sure you know who you're getting involved with first!

Lilly's advice

It's not like I want to scare people off going on dates or anything, because I know I was unlucky and it hasn't put me off trying again. Matt was just the wrong boy to have gone out with. He was bad news altogether. I would say to other girls that it's wise to find out a bit more about the boy before you go off on your own with him. Since I've told people about that night I've heard some weird stories about Matt that might have put me off him if I'd known before. One girl said he was probably sniffing glue as well and he's always been out of order with his girlfriends, yet if you looked at him you couldn't help but feel attracted because he's so nice looking. I know that the next time I go out with a boy (and I hope there is a next time!) I can suss him out a bit better before I decide the attraction is more than just physical.

Contacts

Youth Access   Tel: 01509 210420
Phone between 9 a.m. and 5 p.m. weekdays for details of your nearest Youth Counselling Service.

National Drugs Helpline   Tel: 0800 776600
24-hour confidential advice if you need more information on drugs and solvent abuse.

"MY BEST FRIEND'S TO BLAME FOR MY ANOREXIA"

Photograph posed by model

"I dreaded lunchtimes. She'd have the whole canteen laughing at me!"

16-year-old Claudia had always been happy with her body, until her best friend Mary's cruel comments made her think she should perhaps lose some weight. The bullying and humiliation that followed soon led to life-threatening anorexia and now Claudia wants to share her story to warn other girls of the dangers of dieting ...

I changed schools when I was 14 because my grades were slipping and Mum thought I should start afresh somewhere new before I took GCSEs. When I started there I found the other girls really distant and unfriendly, so I couldn't believe my luck when I

recognized one of my classmates, Mary, from Italian school. (As both our families come from there we went every weekend to learn more about the language and culture.)

Mary was so friendly, showing me around and introducing me to people, that I just latched on to her and we soon became best friends. She was very popular and pretty, and it wasn't long before I had dropped all my mates from my old school for her.

> "I soon realized it was safer to be Mary's friend than her enemy"

Everything was great for that first school year but looking back, there were incidents that should have hinted at what Mary was really like. She was rich and spoiled and although she was the most popular girl in the year, she could also be very cruel, even to people's faces. Somehow she always got away with it and I soon realized it was safer to be Mary's friend than her enemy.

I remember when Mary announced she was going on a diet. She was quite well built but I wouldn't say she was overweight. I was the slimmer one, really. At 5'2", I weighed seven and a half stone and I'd always liked the way people thought of me as petite. I was happy with the way I looked, but from that day on things went downhill.

It seemed to me that Mary loved herself but her weight was the one thing she would like to change. For no good reason she started using me to make her feel better, and constantly commented on how much I was eating. She'd tell the others I was really greedy and take the mickey by making noises like a pig when she mentioned my name. It wasn't long before I dreaded lunchtimes because she'd have the whole canteen looking at me and laughing. Although I never had a massive lunch it seemed like loads more than her lettuce and carrots so I decided to diet too.

> "I'd set the alarm for three in the morning and exercise for two hours"

During the summer I went to Italy to stay with my Grandma. I'd been thinking maybe I *was* a greedy cow, so that first week I started my new regime. I'd only ever eat fruit but even that didn't seem like enough. And when I thought of school I'd feel down and drift off to thinking about food or what I was going to cut down on next. I'd set the alarm for three in the morning and exercise for two hours in secret, then sleep till Grandma woke me and jog round the block a few times before 'breakfast'.

Of course, Grandma nagged me to eat, but if she made me a sandwich I'd bin it as soon as she'd gone out. Then my aunts decided to give a dinner in my honour, which was awful. Traditional Italian food can be packed with calories, so when they brought out an enormous lasagne with melted cheese all over it I just burst out crying. I tried to put the food up my sleeves with my family at the table, that's how desperate I felt.

That night I felt bad even thinking about sitting near all that food, so I started taking laxatives too. I got so ill that Grandma rang home to say I wasn't eating, but it was still a shock for Mum when she picked me up at the airport and I'd lost a stone and a half in the space of the summer ...

"Dieting had turned into a competition to see who could lose most weight"

When I started the new term things got worse. Dieting had turned into a competition to see who could lose most weight in our year and I swear at one point there were only about 10 girls out of 60 eating properly. We'd boast about how little we'd eaten but it was easy to get obsessed when Mary would go on at me for eating an apple. At home, I'd weigh myself on my digital scales every hour and freak if I'd gained even 100 grammes. My periods stopped, my lips went blue, I was always cold and my hair was straggly and thin. I hated myself, so when I looked in the mirror I'd think my cheeks were a bit chubby, or my thighs could be slimmer...I decided to aim for a target weight of 4 stone.

By now I'd been taken to the doctor's and I also went to hospital as an out-patient a couple of times a week. I'd have therapy – sometimes Mum and Dad would take part too – and they'd check on my weight. If I'd lost anything they would ask why, so I'd think to myself, 'You have to eat, Claudia.' Then I'd get to school and see the others starving themselves and of course Mary still went on about her diet. I'd noticed she never got as thin as I did and now I realize she probably went home and ate normally ...

I kept dieting because she would call out the calories and fat grammes in my food in front of the whole school to humiliate me. I had a minimum safe weight so when I hit that the hospital told me I couldn't go home again. I was screaming and crying but they eventually got me into a bed. I was put on a 're-feeding' programme to gain 85% of lost body weight and

I had to be supervised wherever I went, including the loo. I *still* managed to get rid of the food by spitting it out, or dropping it into plastic bags under my clothes. Then I'd drink loads of water before I got weighed, or hide keys in my pockets to make up a few grammes. I lost another half stone and was transferred to a specialist anorexic clinic.

> "If the weight didn't go on I'd be spoon fed"

Everyone at the new place had an eating disorder and there was real pressure to gain at least a kilo every week. The staff didn't mess around there: if the weight didn't go on I'd be spoon fed, and there was always the threat that they'd pipe liquidized food through tubes going down my nose. So slowly the weight went on and I got out just a few weeks ago, five months after admission. I'm almost back to the weight I was at the start.

I went back to school for the first time yesterday and I think I saw a glimpse of Mary at one point. I really don't know what's going to happen the first time we meet because we haven't been in contact. I did get one letter from her, but it was full of how great everything was for her, so I threw it away. As soon as I've passed my GCSEs I'll get out of here and move away to college. Then I'll never see her again.

Therapists focus on my family life because, admittedly, I haven't always got on well with my dad, but I still blame Mary. I can't even say it's all over because if Mum left me alone I'd lose the weight, and quickly too. All I want to do is eat something without thinking what it's doing or where it's going. That's my goal in life because I'm determined not to let Mary win.

Diets: Are you in danger?

Claudia's story shows how easy it can be to take a diet too far. How important is looking thin to you? Does your attitude to eating mean you could be putting your own health at risk? Try our quiz and test your attitudes …

1. Imagine your best friend told you she was starting a strict diet, and she suggested you did the same so you could compare notes. How would you react?
a You'd tell her you'll support her, but you think it's a bad idea to go on a diet just to keep her company.
b You'd make the effort for a couple of weeks, but before long you'd be back to your old eating habits.
c You'd be really into the idea. Competition is a great way to make you want to succeed.

2. You're going to a family wedding in a couple of weeks, but you've just tried on the dress you bought for it ages ago and it's a bit of a squeeze. What are you most likely to do now?
a Go back to the shop to see if they'll exchange the dress for a bigger size.
b Try a few aerobics classes and make a conscious effort to hold your stomach in on the big day.
c Go on a strict diet from now until the wedding – the less you eat the better you'll look in that dress.

3. How do you feel when you look at supermodels on the catwalk?
a You think they look like they could do with a good meal. What's the point of suffering to look so thin?

b You know you'll never look that skinny but maybe you could do with losing a pound here or there.
c Totally depressed but sure that you'll look just as thin if you make a bit of effort.

4. You and your friends have got together to watch videos on Friday night. Everyone's pigging out. What are you doing?
a Trying to sneak that last handful of M&M's before anyone else notices you've eaten the lot.
b Refusing that bit of pizza and feeling a bit guilty about how much you've scoffed already.
c Sipping iced water wondering if none of the others care what they'll look like after this lot.

5. If you were to look in a full-length mirror, completely naked, you'd probably think ...
a "Not perfect, but it's the only body I've got!"
b "Could do with a bit of toning up here and there. Erm ... starting Monday."
c "Yuk! It's still nowhere near the shape I would like it to be."

(27)

6. The best way to get the body you're happy with is to ...
a Make sure you're happy with the rest of you first.
b Be prepared to make sacrifices if you want to change it for the better.
c Make sure it's thinner and better than anyone else's body.

7. In the last year, how often have you thought that you should perhaps cut down on the amount you're eating?
a Hardly ever – there are so many other things to worry about.

b Occasionally, but that doesn't mean that you've stopped eating whatever you like.

c All the time, and you've managed to put your plans into action too.

8. A boy you fancy comments that he thinks you've put a bit of weight on. How do you react?

a You laugh and say he's probably right, but your weight really is none of his business.

b You feel embarrassed that he's noticed and annoyed that you can't get that diet together.

c You're absolutely devastated. If *he* thinks that, what's everyone else saying?

How did you score?

Answered our body image questions honestly? Tot up your score for our quiz (mostly a, b or c) and look below to discover if you too could be in danger from dieting ...

If you scored mostly a

You're lucky enough to have a well balanced attitude to eating, so that means you probably have a well balanced diet too. You know that crash diets are not the answer to a weight problem, but you seem to be happy with your body the way it is, no matter how much you weigh. Slimming isn't a big concern of yours, and if you continue to eat sensibly and take exercise too it shouldn't have to be.

If you scored mostly b

You may feel bothered by your weight at times, but keeping an eye on what you eat seems such a pain that you're not likely to get obsessed. Make sure you don't have the chance to let your body rule your life by aiming for a healthy lifestyle rather than following a strict diet. The trick to keeping in shape is to combine regular exercise with low-fat meals but without torturing yourself over things you think you shouldn't have. If that bar of chocolate makes you feel good then why deny yourself?

If you scored mostly c
Dieting is probably a big part of your life. Can you remember the last time you ate anything without worrying about how it was going to affect your body? Are you sure you really need to lose weight? Don't rely on friends to tell the truth, check with your GP and if you do agree weight loss is a good idea then take things very slowly, following a diet plan approved by him/her. You shouldn't have to punish yourself or put your health at risk to keep in shape.

Anorexia: the facts

What is anorexia?

Anorexia ('the slimmer's disease') is a psychological condition – in other words, the root of the problem is in the sufferer's mind, rather than body. She'll starve herself to get the figure she wants and become obsessed with food in general, counting calories and often eating the same thing day in, day out. Doctors believe anorexics like the feeling of control they have over their eating habits – perhaps they don't have that level of control in other problem areas of their lives. The condition usually affects teenage girls who start with the desire to have a 'perfect body' but soon take the diet further and further until they are scared to lose that feeling of power or gain the tiniest bit of weight.

What are the signs to look for?

If you think you, or a friend, may be at danger of being anorexic, these are some of the warning signs to look out for.

Anorexic people may:

- Count calories obsessively.
- Check their weight more than once a day.
- Lie about how little they have eaten.
- Love to cook elaborate meals for other people – but never eat any themselves.
- Still believe they look fat, even after serious weight loss.
- Wear baggy clothes to hide weight loss.
- Hate to eat with other people present.

Advice

If it's happening to you

Please talk to someone before the situation takes over your life. This isn't a problem you can tackle by yourself, so ask a friend, teacher or parent for help. You can also talk to your GP, ChildLine or the Samaritans for *confidential* advice. Also, there are agencies specially set up to help people in your situation. You are not alone, so please look at our contact addresses overleaf and *act now*. Anorexia can kill.

If it's happening to a friend

She will not be very willing to discuss the problem and it's unlikely that she'll want you to interfere with the situation. You must tell other people – either her parents or a teacher – what you suspect is happening. Although it feels like snitching, anorexia can be a life-threatening condition, and you will be doing her a favour by asking for help on her behalf.

Claudia's advice

If anyone bullies you because of your eating, get away from them even if you think it would take confidence you don't feel you have at the moment. And to those people who might suspect a friend is anorexic then please tell their parents or the school before it gets really out of hand. You could mention to her that you'd noticed she looked a bit down, and she might feel like she can talk to you then. If you're a proper friend then you really should say something because this isn't a problem you should ignore.

Contacts

ChildLine
Tel: 0800 1111 (24 hour telephone counselling)

Eating Disorders Association
Sackville Place, 44–48 Magdalen Street, Norwich NR3 1JE
Tel: 01603 621414
Support and information on self-help groups.

Anorexia and Bulimia Care
15 Fenhurst Gate, Aughton, Lancashire L39 5ED
or
'Arisaig', Back Lane, Monks Eleigh, Suffolk IP7 7BA
Christian organization for help with eating disorders.

Please write to the address nearest to you for more information.

The Samaritans
Tel: 0345 909090 (local rates)
Available 24 hours a day to listen and give advice.

When writing to any of the above contacts for information, please don't forget to enclose a stamped addressed envelope.

"MY HOLIDAY ROMANCE LEFT ME HEARTBROKEN"

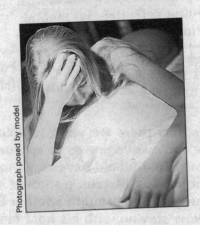

Photograph posed by model

"I knew Peter and I were just perfect for each other"

When Abbie, 17, had a passionate holiday romance, she didn't think for one moment she would be devastated by the events to follow. From now on she will definitely think twice about finding love in the sun ...

Last year I went to France for a fortnight in the summer to stay with a family and study at the local language school. Although I was scared about going off by myself, I shouldn't have worried because everyone was so friendly. There were people from all over the world and it really was the most amazing mix of

cultures and personalities. I was sharing rooms with an Austrian girl, Karinne, and we really hit it off straight away.

> "There was definitely no instant attraction or love at first sight"

> "I realized we had loads in common and he seemed like an old friend"

On my first day there we went to a college party with Karinne and everyone was so approachable and chatty, I didn't feel I would have to sit in the corner feeling self-conscious. Marcus, a student in one of my classes, came over and brought another English boy, Peter, who was staying with his host family too. He had long dark hair and lovely big brown eyes, but there was definitely no instant attraction or love at first sight. I actually thought he was a bit aloof, but decided that was because he was a bit older; 27 in fact. We started chatting and Peter explained that he was from an English family living in Hong Kong and he was staying at the college for the entire summer. From the beginning we realized we had loads in common and I felt almost like he was an old friend.

At the end of the night everyone went back to Marcus and Peter's house and we all sat around for a while, chatting. Before long, I looked round and everyone seemed to have gone and Peter and I were left alone – in his bedroom! He suggested I stay the night in his bed and he would sleep on the floor. I couldn't understand what he wanted because he hadn't even tried to get off with me and I thought he must just want to be friends. I stayed though, and I remember lying there in the darkness wondering if I was meant to make a move on him.

Next morning, Peter went off to get breakfast and when he came back I was singing along to the radio. He put his arm round me and said, 'Calm down, Abbie, you'll wake everyone else up.' Then he kissed me. All I could think about was that even though I liked him a lot I shouldn't have a holiday romance, but I'd made that decision a bit too late. I'd met someone already and I'd been in France for less than 24 hours!

> "I'd only dealt with spotty 17-year-olds before –
> Peter seemed so mature in comparison"

Everyone at college quickly realized that Peter and I were an item because we spent every moment together. It felt so easy and comfortable to be with him, everything was perfect. I'd only ever dealt with spotty 17-year-old boys before and he seemed so romantic and mature by comparison. By the middle of the first week Peter had already admitted that he thought he was falling in love with me, which had me absolutely gobsmacked. There I was, in the most romantic place in the world with a good-looking man who was kind, generous and romantic. I just couldn't believe my luck! I knew I had never felt this way before about anyone, but I felt like everything was happening so quickly it must all be a dream.

One day Peter and I walked around the town and sat in the sunshine drinking champagne. On the way back to my flat he bought me a massive bunch of flowers and I was as happy as I had ever been in my life. I started thinking about our relationship and decided out of the blue that I was going to sleep with

35

him that night. I thought to myself that I was never going to meet anyone else like Peter and I knew that he cared about me deeply and I felt the same way back.

So I stayed over at his place again that night and as usual Peter was on the floor and I had the bed. This time I said to him that if he felt uncomfortable he could get in beside me. That was it – one thing led to another and I lost my virginity that night. The sex was great and I knew we were just perfect for each other.

Next morning I wondered if I had made a really big mistake to get so close to Peter because I was feeling so bad about saying goodbye. I wanted to talk to him about going back home but I think we were both pushing it to the back of our minds. We didn't want the holiday to end, so we tried to block our 'other lives' out. I didn't even send a postcard or phone home again for the rest of the fortnight. I thought if I told anyone else about what was happening to me the magic would go away.

> "I sat on the bed and sobbed because I had lost him and only had my memories"

Peter and I spent every moment of the next week together, and on the day I had to leave I thought my heart was going to break. I was sobbing but before he left me he said that no matter what happened we would always have that special time together and that he truly hoped things could work out. He even said that maybe we would get married one day. I sat on my bed and sobbed because I had lost him and only had my memories.

When I got back to school it was almost like I was

grieving, but I was sure everything would be OK because Peter loved me. But although I wrote, I only got a couple of brief phone calls from him and since I knew that he'd soon be going back to Hong Kong I had to wonder if I would ever see him again.

Then, three months later, I got a call from Peter to say he was in London, and would it be all right if he came over? I was stunned because I had no idea he was even in the country. When he arrived we had a passionate reunion and Mum even said that it would be fine for him to stay the night. Everything was like it always was – we were totally and utterly in love. Or at least I thought we were …

When we woke up we were lounging around in bed, chatting. Suddenly Peter got up and started to get dressed and when I asked if he could stay a bit he said he wanted to go. I was sitting there trying to figure him out when he said, 'Look, Abbie. I don't think it's a good idea for us to see each other any more. I don't think it's going to work.' I felt like I had been slapped in the face; I just couldn't believe what I was hearing. He kept getting his stuff together and went on, 'I think last night proved that we're not right for each other.' I didn't know what he meant – I still don't. The only thing I could think of was that he had suddenly realized how big the age gap was when he saw me at home, talking about school and my friends.

Over and over, I just kept asking him *'Why?'* But he gave me the same answer, that we just weren't right together. He also broke the news that he was leaving for Hong Kong the next day and when I asked for his address he said he wouldn't give it to me. I was screaming and crying, but he walked out. I heard the front door shut behind him and that was the last time I ever saw or heard of him.

A year's gone by now and I'm still in shock. I have so many questions I want to ask, although I suppose when I look back now I think of the whole thing as a good learning experience. Peter and I should have split up before we left France and then I wouldn't have had to go through all this heartache. I wouldn't even have minded as much if he had just let things tail off and come to a natural end. What I can't forgive him for is the way he came back into my life for that one night and left me feeling cheap and used. It really is amazing how quickly love can turn to hate when you have been let down so badly and I don't think I will ever understand him or forgive him for what he did to me.

Can you handle a holiday romance?

Do you go off for a fortnight's fun hoping you'll find the love of your life, or is a holiday fling just a bit of fun in the sun? Try our quiz and find out if you'll have a broken heart by the time the summer is over …

1. On the first day at your hotel you spy the most gorgeous boy you've ever seen in reception. You decide there and then that …

a You've just sussed out your lucky holiday snog for this fortnight.

b You won't be mentioning *him* to your boyfriend back home.

c It might be sunstroke, but you've just fallen in love at first sight.

2. You do a bit of detective work and find out that he doesn't speak much English. That's ...

a A good excuse to have a laugh when you attempt to chat him up.

b A good excuse not to have to write to him after the holiday.

c A good excuse to kiss instead of talk. "I love you" are the only words that count, anyway!

3. There he is in the bar! You're dressed to the nines and this is the perfect opportunity to make him notice you. The easiest way to do that is to ...

a Get him up for a dance next time they play the Birdie Song.

b Get your mates to help you go over and chat to him and his friends.

c Give him a sultry stare over your pina colada, until he gets the message.

4. You eventually get together with your holiday heart-throb. After an evening's snogging you're left wondering ...

a If you could get away with going out with that nice waiter in the hotel restaurant too.

b If you're going to regret this when you get home. After all, you weren't looking for love, were you?

c If you'll live in his country or the UK when you get married and have your eight kids.

5. Your friends and family ask if you can all go out for a night together, because they want to get to know your holiday romance too. What's your reaction?

a The more the merrier – it'll be a right laugh with everyone together.

b Wary. You'd better cool it a bit because you don't

want to make a show of yourself by being all over him.

c A bit miffed because you'd much rather spend what little time you've got totally alone with him.

6. You decide to give him something to remember you by before the time comes to go home again. What's the best goodbye gift you can think of?

a To chuck him into the pool with all his clothes on.

b To leave him with a little note to say thanks for some nice memories.

c To lock yourselves in your hotel room and have a raunchy time he won't forget in a hurry.

7. When you get home again the first thing you want to do is ...

a Find out where you stand with the lads you fancy at home.

b Forget you ever had a fling on holiday. What were you thinking of?

c Get your romantic snaps developed and cry for your lost love.

8. You try to ring the number he gave you before you left each other. When the phone's answered it turns out to be a Chinese takeaway and they have never heard of your holiday love. What's your reaction?

a You think it's hilarious, especially as you gave him the number for your local launderette.

b Disappointed, but it makes things less complicated this way.

c Totally devastated by the whole episode. He must have got his numbers mixed up!

If you scored mostly a

To you, holiday romances are all part of the fun of being away from the rat race. In fact, if you didn't have at least one snog when you were away from home the holiday wouldn't be complete. But what about those boys you leave in your wake – are they the ones who'll be broken-hearted when you jet off back to Britain? Heartbreaker!

If you scored mostly b

There's probably something, or someone, stopping you from letting go completely on holiday. It might be a feeling of guilt because you don't want to mess up another relationship or maybe you just can't be bothered with heartbreak when you have to say goodbye. Either way, you won't take holiday love too seriously, and if you do have a snog it will be almost forgotten by the time you unpack.

If you scored mostly c

We're surprised you had time to complete this quiz. You're probably still staring at photos and cuddling the Spanish donkey your holiday romeo gave you ... from your holiday three years ago! You are convinced love will win over anything, even thousands of miles, massive phone bills and the fact that he was snogging another girl by the time you left for the airport. Enjoy your next holiday romance just as much, but make sure your hopes aren't set too high when you set foot on home soil again.

Advice

If you find love under the sun...

Enjoy it while it lasts

If you meet the boy of your dreams at the start of the holiday you might even get a bit upset about long-distance love while you're still there! Don't let your thoughts dwell on the inevitable goodbye, because it's got to come eventually. You'll only have memories when you get home again, so try to make them as happy as possible.

Don't rush the relationship

When time is running out you might feel the pressure to make him realize how serious your feelings are. Telling him how you feel is one thing, but what about the temptation to take the relationship further than you would have done with a more normal relationship at home? Well, sex is more risky on holiday, partly because you don't know much about your partner or his history and partly because you're probably rushing into things before you're really ready. Leave the hot stuff at sunbathing – you won't regret it.

Protect yourself

Sun and sangria can make you throw caution to the wind and forget about essential things like protecting yourself both from pregnancy and from HIV and other sexually transmitted diseases. You never know what's going to happen on holiday so make sure you buy condoms in this country and take them abroad with you.

Get the information you need

Come the end of the summer, magazines like MIZZ get the same sort of letters all the time. Heartbroken readers ask if we can put them in touch with "Steve from the Midlands – I don't know his second name, but we fell in love …" If you are even in with a chance of a reunion with your holiday romance, make sure you get all the right addresses and numbers, and give him yours too.

Get on with your life at home

When you get home again the temptation is to lock yourself away, stare at the photos and get depressed about how boring life is compared to your fortnight in the sun. The easy way to get out of the depression is to give your social life a kick-start now you are home again. Get out there and you might find a lad closer to home who could put your sizzling summer love in the shade!

Know how to handle heartbreak

Not what you want to hear, we know, but holiday romances very rarely work out. If you live too far away then you have to get on with your own lives too and that sometimes means finding another, more accessible partner. So we don't want to dash your dreams, but don't rest all your hopes on making long-distance love work. As well as the problems of travel there can be cultural differences, language problems, not to mention family opposition to beat. Good luck with keeping summer love strong all the year through – you're going to need it!

Abbie's advice

"I wouldn't ever have another holiday romance personally, but that's because things didn't work out for me first time around. Of course, you try to tell yourself that your relationship will be one of the few that overcome the problems of long-distance love, but things very rarely work out. To anyone else hoping to meet someone and fall in love on holiday, I wish you luck. Being swept off your feet is an experience, but remember just to live for the moment and enjoy your fling – after all it's an experience! Hard as it is, you have to think about what's going to happen when you get back: if you think there's even a vague possibility that it won't work, then be friends when you leave and even still contact each other, but don't expect romance to last."

Contacts

If you've lost your holiday romeo's address you're probably at a loss about what to do. Why not try a request on **local radio** in his area? It might work, but only broadcast if you're sure he won't have a wife and kids tuning in!

"HOW I COPED WHEN MY TWIN SISTER DIED"

Photograph posed by model

"The pain is worse when I'm on my own and I think about her all the time"

Natasha and her twin sister Elisa would have been celebrating their 17th birthday together last July. But just days before, Elisa became dangerously ill and died of meningitis. Natasha's grief has been hard to cope with at times, but she wants to tell her story to help other people come to terms with the pain of losing a loved one ...

Elisa and I were identical twins and looked exactly alike, or we did until we were about 12. Then we decided that we wanted to cultivate our own personalities and dress differently, but we still got on really well and we loved each other's company. Of course there were bad patches, but we had the same likes and dislikes, and the same friends, and loved being together constantly. We were even told we'd have to stop sharing a bedroom because we laughed and talked too much when we were together.

> "We had so many shared thoughts and ambitions"

I remember the first time Elisa ever stayed over at a friend's house I felt really strange, as though there was something really important missing. I felt lost without her. But I realized we had to grow up and lead separate lives sometime so we always said that we wouldn't go to the same universities when we got older. Even at that, we agreed we'd probably stay in the same house after we graduated. We talked about going on a skiing trip one day because Mum and Dad had never fancied it much, so we thought it was something we'd do together when we were older. We had so many shared thoughts and ambitions. We even dreamt the same things and one night both had bad dreams that the other twin would die. I never thought that one day the nightmare would become reality.

It all started one Sunday five days before our 17th birthday. In the morning Elisa was her usual self, laughing and joking about something and messing around. But then, after dinner, she came into my room and told me she felt really shaky and cold, like she was getting flu. I told her I'd warm her up and gave her a big hug, then suggested she read a book to take her mind off how awful she felt. But it didn't do any good, and she went downstairs to tell Mum she was feeling even worse. As Elisa had a raging temperature and kept being sick, Mum put her in bed and then rang the doctor. He said it sounded like bad flu and Elisa should be kept in bed. But during the night she got so bad that she couldn't walk to the toilet and Mum noticed she was starting to get red patches all over her skin. We called the doctor out and he took one look at my sister and phoned for an ambulance, saying that he thought she had meningitis and septicaemia, which is a form of blood poisoning. As the ambulancemen took Elisa away she said to me, 'Look at my skin, what's happening?' and I told her not to worry because she'd be fine. I hugged her and that was the last time I ever spoke to her ...

> "It didn't look very promising, but inside I couldn't believe it"

47

Mum went with Elisa, who was slipping into unconsciousness. I'd been told not to go in to school, and later on Mum called home to say that it looked quite bad and that we had better get to the hospital. The whole family stayed with her until late that night, then me, my gran and my other sister Catherine went home to wait for news while Mum and Dad stayed at Elisa's bedside in intensive care. I had to ring Elisa's best friend and tell her what had happened and that it didn't look very promising, but inside I couldn't believe it. I was certain she would be all right again, absolutely certain.

> "It was very upsetting to see her like that and I still have nightmares about it"

> "I could hear the long beep of her heart monitor and I knew she had gone"

Mum rang again to say that they were pumping antibiotics into Elisa and that now her kidneys weren't working and she wasn't getting rid of all the fluids and toxins. She was dying. When we got to the hospital again I was shocked to see that she was all bloated and didn't look like my sister at all. It was very upsetting to see her like that and I still have nightmares about it. Mum told me she was slipping away and that was so scary, but it was like it wasn't happening. I wanted to tell Elisa I needed her and that she couldn't go, I wouldn't let her. But at 4 p.m. that afternoon she died, just as the doctor had told us to go in to be with her for her last few moments. As I walked towards her room I could hear the long beep of her heart monitor and knew she had already gone. The doctors allowed us to sit with her for a while, though they made us put on masks and aprons so we didn't catch an infection. We all got our chance to say goodbye and I'll always be grateful for that.

I was numb when I got home again. I was walking around in a daze and almost thought to myself that Elisa was on holiday and was going to come back. I can't remember how I felt – maybe I didn't feel anything, because I know it took me at least a couple of months to cry about it. Even then I would never break down in front of other people, only alone in my room or when I was with Mum.

I went into school after a couple of days, to see friends at lunchtime rather than go to lessons. Some of them looked at me, smiled and said how sorry they

48

were, but apparently a teacher had said that if pupils weren't in our close group of friends then they shouldn't all crowd round me and make a fuss. I noticed some people felt awkward, so I made an effort to seem happy and easy to approach. People cried a lot and it was very much like I was the one comforting them. I'm told it's often like that.

The following week we had Elisa's funeral and lots of fellow pupils came along to that, though we'd already had a memorial service in school. Mum, Dad, Catherine and I were able to see Elisa before the funeral and I felt a lot better being able to see her one last time. We played her favourite Michael Jackson song and gave readings from her favourite books, which everyone found very moving.

For the first couple of months I didn't feel much and I almost think it's got harder to cope as time goes by because Elisa was such a good influence on me and encouraged me to work harder at school and so on. It's so difficult on my own, but my friends have been excellent, especially at Christmas and on special occasions when I miss her a lot. Though our birthday was just after Elisa died, our friends still came round to see me and we had a barbecue, like we'd done every other year. People were so nice to me.

Losing Elisa has changed the way I look at my life. I don't get cross with others so much – there are more important things to worry about. I still want to do the things we talked about together. For example, she was always on at me to book driving lessons after our 17th birthday, so I did that because Elisa would have wanted me to. We've got photos of her all round the house and I'm always looking at them. The pain is worse when I'm on my own and I think about her all the time because there was never a day when I didn't have her there with me.

That's what's been so difficult to accept, but I will never forget my sister. I know I'm not the only one. **"**

Can you help a friend in need?

If you don't have the experience of having someone close to you die, it can be hard to know how to help a mate who is trying her best to cope. Try our test and you'll find out more about how you can help ease the pain and lend your support ...

1. When your friend brings up the subject of the person who has died the best thing for you to do is ...
a Listen.
b Try to change the subject.

2. When you see your friend for the first time after they've been bereaved, the best thing you can do is ...
a Avoid the subject of their bereavement at all costs.
b Say something about the death as soon as you meet.

3. Your friend and her family would probably appreciate ...
a A quick call to ask if there's anything you can do to help.
b A bit of peace and quiet with no interference from people outside the family.

4. When should your friend have started to get over the grief?
a After about six months.
b Probably never.

5. If you do write a card or letter, it's more comforting to …
a Include a little note sharing some memories.
b Simply sign your name rather than write a message.

6. If you're one of the first people to find out what's happened, you should …
a Keep the news to yourself.
b Let other people know as soon as possible.

Answers

1. (a) Listen. It's important to let them know you are there if they'd like to talk about their feelings, or about the person who has died, even if you didn't know them. It can be comforting to talk about their memories, good and bad.

2. (b) Say something. Don't avoid bringing up the subject when you first meet for fear of 'reminding' your friend about their grief. It's very unlikely they'll have forgotten and letting them know you're aware of the situation and that you're ready to lend support could be a great help.

3. (a) A quick call. Why not ask if her family would like you to help with practical things? It could be anything from offering to sort out shopping to keeping an eye on pets when they attend the funeral, but every little bit helps.

4. (b) Probably never, although she will improve as time goes by. Don't lose patience with your friend if you feel it's taking too long for her to get over the grief. The last thing she needs is other people thinking she should 'pull herself together'. Take more time to listen and talk things over.

5. (a) Write a note, saying how sorry you are to hear the sad news. If you knew the person who died, you might like to share some memories you have of that person, but remember to mention that the letter does not need to be answered. When your mate feels bad she'll probably look at messages like these again and they'll help her realize she's not alone.

6. (b) Let other people know. You don't want to spread gossip about your friend's bereavement, but if you are one of the first to know it might be a good idea to let her closer friends know what's happened. Is she likely to be taking time off school? Have a word with her form teacher and make sure she's aware of the reasons too.

Advice

Coping with grief

When someone close to you has died, it's only natural that you should go through a whole range of emotions. You're likely to feel ...

Shocked even if you knew that the person you've lost had been very ill. Perhaps the news was broken to you in an upsetting way, or you feel that you will never really get over the grief that you feel now. Although it sounds corny, people will tell you time helps you to come to accept death and you will 'get over it' in a while. Well, perhaps you never will accept what has happened, but time really will help you to handle your feelings better.

Angry, perhaps with the person you're grieving over, perhaps because of the manner in which they died. Why didn't they look after their health more? Why did they take risks? How could they leave you like this? Perhaps you are angry with yourself that you didn't prevent the death or are somehow to blame? It pays to talk about your feelings with a good friend or even a trained counsellor because these feelings may not be easy to shake off.

Isolated because you feel you have been left to cope alone with your feelings. It's possible you may not want to share your grief with your friends and family because you don't want to upset them more if they are grieving too. We all like to be alone with our thoughts and emotions, but it's not always healthy to hide them away from those close to you. Remember that they too will be suffering.

Sleepless because thoughts of that person keep going through your head. You may also have lost your appetite and find it hard to concentrate on the tiniest thing. These are very like the symptoms of depression, and if you haven't got into a more normal routine and sleep pattern after a while, it might be advisable to go and see your GP for further help, or to ask that he recommend a counsellor in your area.

Disinterested in all the other things happening in your life. It can be difficult to function from day to day when you feel as though the world has come to an end. You may even lose touch with friends because you don't feel like going out and having fun, and because you believe that mates can't possibly feel sympathy when they haven't experienced the same kind of grief.

Impatient with your friends because they're not giving you the support or understanding that you need at this difficult time. Don't hide yourself away and lose touch with good mates now. Try to tell them how you feel and what they can do to help you cope better, then they'll be sure to help in any way they can.

Natasha's advice

If you block things out you'll make things harder for yourself in the long run. You might find that all of a sudden the pain builds up and that's not good for you, so my advice is to talk about the way you feel. Make yourself approachable and talk to other people. You will get used to your grief and find your own ways to cope.

Try to remember the person you've lost in any way you can. We planted a tree at school in Elisa's memory and there's a little marble plaque on the wall beside it with her name on, so she'll always be remembered at school. It's nice to know that her name is still around.

If you are a friend of someone who has recently been bereaved, please don't avoid that person because you think you're going to upset them. You won't upset them by just chatting and being friendly. Not only will your friend want to talk about the person who has died, she'll want to talk about other, everyday things too, and will need your help to get on with her own life.

I got some lovely letters and poems which really

helped a lot, so it's good idea to send a note if you can. I still have the cards I was sent after Elisa died and it always helps to have a look at them when I'm feeling down. "

Contacts

Cruse Bereavement Care
Cruse House, 126 Sheen Road, Richmond, Surrey TW9 1UR.
Write to this address, or look for your local group in your phone book. They offer a special phone counselling service, Bereavement Line (0181 332 7227). Cruse have regional support groups and should be able to put you in touch with local support.

Your GP may be able to recommend self-help groups in your area, or check in your local library for more details of local counselling.

British Association for Counselling (BAC)
1 Regent Place, Rugby, Warwickshire CV21 2PJ
Tel: 01788 578328
Publishes lists of counselling organizations and individual counsellors and psychotherapists throughout the UK.

When writing to any of the above, please don't forget to enclose a stamped, addressed envelope.

"BULLIES BEAT ME - BUT I'M FIGHTING BACK"

Photograph posed by model

"They didn't just bully me - that's not a strong enough way to describe it"

Melanie is 17 and lives in Scotland. She has struggled to come to terms with her traumatic school life but feels determined that bullying classmates won't ruin her future ...

There was always a group of four boys and three girls who went about together at school, and even from first year I knew they were trouble. I managed to get to second year without them picking on me, but then, for no good reason they latched on to me because I was quiet and wouldn't stick up for myself. They started to make my life a misery.

> "When the teacher wasn't looking, the boy would order me to undo the zip on my trousers"

They didn't just bully me, that's not a strong enough way to describe it. They abused me mentally, physically and sexually. I hated the thought of going to school, especially when any of them were in my classes, because one of the boys would sit beside me and when the teacher wasn't looking he'd order me to undo the zip on my trousers, saying that he'd beat me up if I didn't. I'd do it through fear, and the teacher would never notice. If she turned the other way he would try to put his hands down my trousers. Some of my mates would notice what was happening and would never stick up for me because they were scared too.

> "They said that if I dared to tell anyone what was happening they would kill me"

It was even worse outside school. They'd get me on the way home and would drag me into a golf course beside the school and make me pull my trousers and pants down because one of the blokes said he wanted to have sex with me. He never did, but once they nearly got caught by a man walking his dog who shouted out and asked what we thought we were doing. The bullies ran off and I was left there trying to get dressed again. When I got up, the man had gone, so they all came over to me again and said that if I dared to tell anyone about what was happening then they would kill me – and I believed them because I knew a couple of the boys had knives.

> "My hair was falling out in clumps because of the worry"

When I got home, my gran had my dinner ready as usual and I had to make another excuse why I was late – because school was only a five minute walk away. In fact, the whole family was starting to notice there was something wrong, because if anyone spoke to me I was usually in a world of my own or staring into space. I'd jump if any of them touched me. Mum was always asking if there was anything bad happening at school and I always told her there was nothing to worry about, but she didn't believe me. I was scared to brush my hair because it was falling out in clumps because of the worry and I wondered how long I would be able to hide the truth from everyone.

I didn't have to tell the school, because after about three months one of my friends, Marie, did it for me. She said she couldn't bear to see me going through hell any more and told one of our favourite teachers how I was being spat on, laughed at and tripped up in corridors. She thought that was as serious as it got!

It was such a relief that someone in the school knew what was happening to me, and as the teacher took me and my friend into her little office I hoped that everything was going to be all right. She explained that she was going to have to tell the headmaster and so maybe I should go home and tell my family what had been going on as he'd want to talk to them about it too.

The bullies were outside waiting for me as usual

that afternoon and they dragged me behind a wall and made me expose my body to the rest of the school. It was sickening, and they all called me the biggest slag in the school and said I would go with anyone. It just wasn't true and I was so terrified I thought about just going home and killing myself. Instead, I went to my bedroom and cried my heart out so much that my mum came in to see what was wrong and I had to tell her the truth.

It was difficult to get the story out and Mum was really angry when I told her what they had done to me, and annoyed I hadn't been able to tell her sooner. When we went downstairs and she told my gran and grandpa and my uncle, who wanted to go and find the bullies and give them a hiding. Instead, Mum decided we should talk to the police because it was such a serious matter. When they arrived they were nice to me and told me to take my time and say exactly what had happened. They said to stop worrying because everything would be all right now.

When me, Mum and Gran went to see the head we had to wait for a while outside his office and I noticed that a couple of the bullies had come upstairs to collect their conduct sheets from the office next door. They said hello to me and tried to get me on my own, probably to ask why I had my family with me, but I wouldn't go near them. They looked worried, and that gave me some strength. I can't say the headmaster was as helpful as the first teacher I spoke to, but he did sit up and take notice when my gran told him that the police would be coming up to get some statements from the pupils involved.

The case was eventually taken to a Children's Panel court, but because other people in my class were too scared to be witnesses the bullies got away with it.

Their lawyers made out that I had asked for it and they had all got their stories together to make sure they were the same. I had to be strong that day for my mum and the rest of my family because we were all hurting and I was glad in a way to have got things over and done with, even if they hadn't got what they deserved.

> "I deserve to do well after the bad luck I have had in life"

I was still glad I had told the truth, though, and we all decided that I should go to a new school from then on. It took me a while to make new friends and for ages I had to be taken there and back because I was too frightened to travel by myself. The doctor told my mum that I had been through a lot for someone so young and had been about to have a nervous break-down, but I've come through it. Even after everything I have had to endure, I feel good about myself again. I've left school and when I'm not looking for a job I love singing. I even got on television once, so that has kept me going. My family and the few friends I have were so proud of me and say I deserve to do well after the bad luck I have had in life.

When I'm out at shops or whatever I'm always looking over my shoulder for the bullies. Maybe it's a fear that will always be with me, but I've learned that I've got to pick myself up and get on with the rest of my life. I can't let them stop me living, because that would mean they'd won.

Could you beat a bully?

Forget exams – tackling bullies could be the most difficult thing you ever have to do at school. Try our quiz and check the answer pages to see how you can best tackle the problem ...

1. If you want to talk to the headmaster about being bullied it's useful to get prepared before you see him. That means you ...
a Get a gang of friends in there too to stick up for you.
b Drag the bullies in with you to explain themselves.
c Rehearse exactly what you want to say in case you get upset.

2. Bullies often pick on other people because they ...
a Love making people sit up and take notice.
b Have problems of their own they'd rather forget.
c Have violent tempers they can't seem to control.

3. When parents are told their child is being bullied they are usually ...
a Angry that their son or daughter has been getting into trouble.
b Annoyed that now they've got one more thing to worry about.
c Determined to sort things out as soon as possible.

4. If you knew that a bully was waiting for you after school the best way to handle it would be to ...
a Tell a teacher what's going on as soon as you can.
b Organize another way to get home.
c Hide in the school building until a mate can give the all clear.

5. People who are bullied are usually the ones who …

a Are weak and can't stick up for themselves.

b The bullies are jealous of.

c Are unlucky enough to be singled out for no good reason.

6. When it comes to bullying, most schools …

a Have a plan of action that starts as soon as the abuse is reported to them.

b Have to wait until things get really bad before they can threaten the bully with action.

c Try to ignore the fact that there's a problem because it's bad for their image.

7. When a bully threatens to get violent with you, the best thing to do is to …

a Make sure you have witnesses willing to say what they've heard.

b Make sure you're going to hit them harder than they'll hit you.

c Get to safety as fast as you can and tell someone in authority.

63

8. If teachers got involved the bully would most likely …

a Go completely crazy and probably beat you up.

b Ignore you or walk away because they'd be too scared to do anything.

c Get everyone else to fall out with you as punishment.

Check out how you scored. Here we'll go through the answers with you to give some essential advice on how to tackle the big problem of bullying …

1. (c) Rehearse exactly what you want to say in case you get upset.

The first thing you have to do is to make your teacher realize there is a big problem. Details like the 'wheres and whens' can be gone over later. Right now, you have to say who's bullying you and why it's affecting you and your work, so have an idea what details you want to give in your first meeting. Get your point across and your teacher should sit up and take notice.

2. (b) Bullies have problems of their own they would rather forget.

They might seem super-confident and in love with themselves, but underneath it all most bullies have problems in their lives. Maybe they are actually being bullied themselves by parents or their brothers and sisters. Picking on you gives them a way to vent their aggression and to feel in control again.

3. (c) Parents are usually determined to sort things out as soon as possible.

Sometimes, telling parents is the last thing you feel like doing. After all, if you've been bunking school or pretending to be sick to avoid going in, then all that might have to come out too, right? But think about it, no matter what your parents have on their plates already, they'd want to know if you were seriously unhappy. You may also need their help to change the situation because it's a lot to handle on your own.

4. (a) Tell a teacher what's going on as soon as you can.

Yes, that's right – grass, snitch and tell tales! No matter how much you hate the thought of telling others, that really is the only way you can solve the problem of bullying in the long term. Hiding from your enemies will only delay the confrontation and problems like this will wear you down if they worry you for too long. Act as soon as you can, because the bullying is only going to get worse if you ignore it.

5. (c) Victims are unlucky enough to be singled out for no good reason.

Don't think there must be something wrong with you because you are the one the bully has picked on. OK, they might have a personal grudge against you, but it's just as likely that you were in the wrong place at the wrong time and the abuse has carried on from there. Even the most popular pupil can be singled out for no good reason.

6. (a) Most schools have a plan of action that starts as soon as the abuse is reported to them.

You probably won't be the first person to have reported bullying in your school, so teachers may be quite used to dealing with this sort of problem. Most schools now have an anti-bullying policy and are prepared on how to deal with the problem quickly and effectively. After all, they have your welfare (and performance in the classroom) at heart and they want you to be happy at school.

7. (c) Get to safety as fast as you can and tell someone in authority.

Sometimes there's just no arguing with a bully because they'll have made their mind up already that they want to fight. Don't let them lead you into a confrontation – walk away and tell someone what's happening, with witnesses to back you up if that's possible. We all know bullies are usually followed around by a little clique, so with the numbers not in your favour there's not a lot else you can do.

8. (b) They will ignore you or walk away because they are too scared to say anything.
It's amazing how sheepish even the scariest bully can become when they've had a severe dressing down from someone in authority. The bully may not look like they care what they do, but when they know teachers are keeping a close eye on the situation they'd be stupid to get into more trouble. If they know you're keeping note of the bullying and aren't scared to say anything they'll find someone else to bother or, even better, give up altogether. By acting on the problem you could be doing everyone else a favour too!

Advice

66

Our top ten action points ...

1. Speak out now before your situation gets any worse.
2. Trust your teachers to help you. They really are the best people to help remedy the situation.
3. You may be able to help other people who are being hassled by the same bully. Make a stand and help stamp out the problem all over the school.
4. If your parents ask what's wrong, let them know. You are not telling tales, just letting them in on the secret of what's bothering you.
5. Have confidence in yourself. You may be being picked on, but you are not the first person it has happened to, and you're not a failure because

you've got this problem. Give yourself a confidence boost by beating the bullies!

6. Enlist the help of other school mates you know are being picked on too. There's power, as well as safety, in numbers.

7. Rehearse what you want to say when you tell someone for the first time; that way you won't get tongue-tied and walk away yet again, saying "Nothing's the matter ..."

8. Don't take the usual advice to "hit the bully back harder". Instead, put a stop to it once and for all and sort the problem out in the Head's office rather than in Casualty!

9. Keep involved in decisions and make sure teachers keep you updated on how your case is being dealt with.

10. Don't let bullies ruin your life! Concentrate on the other things in your life that you do enjoy and make your mind up now that you won't let them spoil your fun.

Melanie's advice

I hate to hear about anyone being bullied because I know exactly how they feel and what they must be going through. I still think the best thing to do is to tell someone what's happening. Do it as soon as you can, because I've always regretted not saying something sooner. There's someone to help you, so ring ChildLine and ask for some advice – I wish I'd thought of it. Once you realize you can talk to someone you'll never want to stay silent again, and you certainly won't want to take the worst way out and think about ending it all. That won't solve your problem.

The only way to get rid of bullies once and for all is to speak out now, so start by telling your family. That's the only way you are going to mend your self-esteem and get on the road to recovery.

Contacts

Kidscape
152 Buckingham Palace Road, London SW11
Tel: 0171 730 3300
Offers support material to individuals and also to schools for development of anti-bullying policy. They also have a counsellor available to talk to and advise the parents of bullied young people.

Scottish Anti-Bullying Initiative
SCRE, 15 St John's Street, Edinburgh, EH8 8JR

ABC (Anti Bullying Campaign)
10 Borough High Street, London SE1 9QQ

ChildLine
Tel: 0800 1111
Although their special anti-bullying line is no longer open due to lack of funding, they'll still give invaluable advice on how to beat bullies.

Please enclose a stamped addressed envelope in all correspondence.

"MY TEACHER FANCIED ME!"

Photograph posed by model

"The others hadn't guessed how close we were to an affair"

16-year-old Jenna felt so attracted to her science teacher that she decided she wasn't interested in any other boys at school. But when she realized that he might feel the same way back she began to wonder if she was in too deep ...

I left school last year and on my final day my friends and I went round the classrooms to ask for our teachers' autographs as a little memento. When we came out of our third year science room I looked at my book and saw that Mr Wright had written 'See you sometime?' in there. I suppose he couldn't have put

anything more personal because the others hadn't guessed how close we were to getting together a while back ...

> "I suppose I was on the lookout for someone to fancy"

When I was thirteen I was the only one out of my friends who didn't have a boyfriend. Even my mum had been badgering me and asked why I wasn't going out with anyone, so I suppose I was on the lookout for someone to fancy. There were a few boys around, but none of them seemed like anything special.

I loved science and I always got good grades for it, and our teacher, Mr Wright, was always writing comments in my books like 'good work' and 'excellent'. I think it was my friend Carol who first put the idea in my head. During the class one day she'd said, for a joke, 'I think he likes you, you know.' She probably expected me to be horrified at the possibility, but I wasn't. And when I thought about it he did always seem to be around my group whenever we were doing experiments in the class. I'd thought before I was just one of his favourite students, but now I realized it could be more than that.

> "Colin wasn't the sort of teacher all the other girls would have fancied"

Colin wasn't the sort of teacher all the other girls would have fancied: after all he was virtually bald, wore glasses and wasn't very trendy. He must have been in his late thirties – I mean, he was almost three times my age!

So I started to make a bit of an effort to talk to him in class. If we were doing an experiment he would always ask if anyone needed help, and I'd always ask for it even if I was sure of what I was doing. If he made a joke I'd try to answer back and before long he made a point of paying more attention to me than ever.

> "I was relieved to find out he wasn't married"

I always looked forward to Mr Wright's classes and wished I could see him more than twice a week. I was always thinking about him, no matter what class I was in, and before long I decided that I had to find out a bit more about him. I asked around and was relieved to discover he wasn't married, and as far as I knew he didn't have a girlfriend either. I'd also heard that he lived in the town next to ours so I looked for his name in the phone book and then suggested to Carol that we go for a walk around there one day during the summer holidays. She had no idea why I wanted to go, but followed as we walked up the street where he – Colin – lived. To be honest, I was terrified that he was going to bump into me, or look out of his window as we passed, but it felt really good to see where he spent his time out of school. It was just an ordinary bungalow, but now I could visualize him at home.

When I started in fourth year it probably became quite obvious that I liked him a lot. Science was always the last lesson of the day and I would always hang around afterwards hoping that we'd be able to have a chat. I'd take ages to pack my stuff up so I was the last one out. All I wanted to do was to get to know him a bit better and he didn't seem to mind answering me when I asked him quite personal questions, like how old he was and whether he had a girlfriend yet. In fact, he used to ask me the same sort of things too. It was almost like he seemed eager for me to ask more questions and I knew that even if he wasn't interested in me, he didn't mind me fancying him. It was like he had started to lead me on.

> "I decided to keep him as more of a fantasy boyfriend"

There was a problem that kept going round in my head, that he would never really be able to be my boyfriend even if we could have got together. I knew that my parents would never have stood for it because they are strict with me. And I knew I would have got expelled and he would have been disciplined, if not sacked. It was then that I decided to keep him as more of a fantasy boyfriend – someone I could think about and look forward to seeing, but I didn't have to have a real relationship with him. He had other ideas, I think.

It got near Christmas and after the class one day he gave me a note. On the way home I read it and I was really touched that he'd gone to all that trouble for me. He'd written a Christmas poem all about me and although it wasn't exactly lovey-dovey, it did show that he cared a lot. I'd even go and find him at breaks now, and if he was in his classroom I'd sit there with him and we'd chat. He couldn't have thought it was totally innocent, even though he never went further than holding my hand. I couldn't have risked another teacher coming in and catching us kissing. As it was, if someone came in and we were just talking he'd have to pull a book out and pretend he was going over some homework with me.

When he found out it was my 16th birthday he gave me another letter, which turned out to be an invitation to a wedding. When I looked closer, I realized it was something he'd mocked up on the computer and the wedding was *ours*. I was shocked and I think that's when I realized all this was getting a bit too serious and we were in real danger of going too far. I felt scared about how much he liked me, so I went home and threw away the invite along with the other notes he'd given me. I guessed my mum had already found them anyway, because she kept asking how I was getting on with my science lessons and what my teacher was like. Looking back, it was her way of letting me know she suspected. Then other things put me off too. I didn't know, but some of the boys in my science group had seen him passing another note to me and started making little jokes about my 'chemistry' with the science teacher and how he was 'Jenna's Mr Wright'. The rumours started to go round the whole school and I knew we were in a potentially disastrous situation.

Slowly, I stopped hanging around him after classes and I think he got the message. He told me he'd also got an inkling that another teacher had twigged and thought it might be a good idea to see less of each other anyway.

So it tailed off, and I got a boyfriend of my own, which was a lot easier than fancying someone I couldn't ever risk getting together with. I've left school now and I don't think about Colin much. If I bumped into him now I certainly wouldn't fancy him, because I've got a real relationship. He's still at my old school and as far as I know, he's not flirting with any other pupils.

I was the only one he ever did that with, but I'm sure when he looks back he's as relieved as I am that we stopped things before they got properly started.

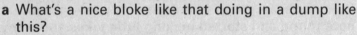

Are you turned on by your teacher?

The thought of romance with a teacher is exciting to some, and enough to make others want to play truant for the rest of their schooldays. Could you ever find love in the classroom? Try our quiz and find out …

1. You're introduced to your new geography teacher – and he looks like he's just walked out of a MIZZ male model shoot. What do you think?

a What's a nice bloke like that doing in a dump like this?

b I'd better get to snog him on the next field trip.

c Bet he's as much of a prat as every other teacher in the school.

2. You're out shopping when you see your favourite teacher browsing through the men's undies in M&S. What do you do?

a Walk past, say hello and try not to collapse laughing when his face goes purple.

b Sidle up secretly for a better look, hoping you can suss what sort of pants he wears.

c Make a mental note to slag him off about it next time you're in his class.

3. If a teacher asked you for a dance at a school disco you would probably …

a Do it for a laugh and hope none of the lads you fancy spotted you.

b Get right in there and hope the next record is a slow one.

c Look at him as though he's dirt and wander off to find some better company.

4. You've never fancied skiing much, but you'd probably consider going on a school trip to the Alps if ...

a All the best-looking boys from the sixth form were going too.

b All the best-looking teachers were there to supervise.

c All the teachers broke something and ended up in hospital.

5. When you watch other girls in the class trying to flirt with a teacher, you ...

a Feel relieved that they're distracted, 'cos meanwhile you can chat to the lads.

b Feel like you have to compete with them for his attention. This isn't fair!

c Feel like throwing up in the corner and wish they'd get a life.

6. You hear about a girl in your form having a supposedly secret affair with one of the teachers at school. What's your reaction?

a Why does she have to go for an old bloke when there are so many other nice boys of her own age?

b How did she manage to do it, and can she share her secret with you?

c You think she must need her head looking at. Isn't there an easier way to get good marks?

7. Do you ever think about your teachers and what sort of life they have outside the school?

a Not particularly – they don't interest you enough to care too much about what they get up to.

b You wonder about everything – what they wear, where they go, their sex lives, their phone numbers ...

c Never. Mind you, you have to wonder if some of them are actually human in the first place.

8. If, like Jenna, your teacher had sent you a poem he'd specially written for you, how would you feel?

a Surprised, but you'd decide not to tell anyone else about it because it could get him into loads of trouble.

b That he must be in love with you and that you can't believe your luck!

c That he must be some sort of weirdo and you're going to tell everyone what's happened!

How did you score?

If you answered mostly a

There's no way you could ever let yourself get involved with a teacher, probably because you're too busy chasing lads of your own age! Getting on well with a teacher is one thing, and you feel quite comfortable being friendly and sharing a joke with him. But fancying him would be totally out of the question because you know there are too many risks involved – and you couldn't find him attractive in the first place.

If you answered mostly b

You will have to be careful not to confuse a bit of attention from a teacher in the classroom with romantic interest. You'll read something into every comment he makes and the encouragement he gives you, but are you sure you are the only one? Even allowing yourself to fancy a teacher could make your life a misery, especially when other people find out – so make sure you are the only person who knows what's going on inside your head!

If you answered mostly c

The last person in the world you would want to get closer to would be a teacher. In fact, there aren't many of them you actually like enough to want to talk to, never mind chat up. School is a place you like to forget as soon as possible after you leave at the end of the day, so the one thing you don't want to do is spend time thinking about the people running it.

Advice

If you fancy your teacher

Don't put him in an awkward situation

If you do fancy your teacher, the last thing you want to do is to tell him how you feel. What's he meant to do, say "I love you too" and whisk you off your feet just as the headmaster walks in? It's better for you both if you keep everything to yourself, so a confrontation is not an option.

Don't let rumours start

It's a very bad idea to start telling other people how you feel, especially friends at the same school. When word gets around not everyone will have a sympathetic viewpoint, especially those who think you're an easy target for loud jokes within earshot of the teacher in question.

Don't exaggerate the truth

So he looked at you in a lesson, or praised you for something? Don't decide that this means he feels the same way back, because the chances are that he's just a good teacher doing his job! So what if he does pay you attention? That's what teachers are there for, so don't try to convince yourself that he fancies you too. Even if you are the class favourite, that doesn't mean you're about to start a torrid affair!

Respect his life outside school

It's fascinating trying to imagine teachers out of school. What kind of social life do they have? Are they in a relationship? What sort of house do they live in? When you do like someone it's normal to want to find out a whole lot more about them, but when that person is a teacher the exploration has to stop at a daydream. Pursuing him outside class is pointless: even if you are both very different beyond the school gates, he will probably never forget he is the teacher and you are the pupil.

Don't flirt

You can customize your uniform, give the wittiest answers in class and make cheeky comments in discussion groups – but even if your teacher does notice that you are making a special effort for him it's more likely to embarrass than attract him.

Don't build up your hopes

You have to face the fact that you two are almost certainly not going to get together. There's one tricky problem when it comes to a teacher telling you that he thinks you're not half bad yourself ... he'll lose his job for it. Teacher/pupil relationships are totally forbidden in schools and so he could fancy you loads, but won't be likely to risk his livelihood for you.

If it works, it can wait

If you seriously think you could have something going with a teacher, then wait until you have left school for good before you get together. That way his job isn't in jeopardy and you'll have loads of time to think about whether it's a wise move in the first place.

If he fancies you ...

Lechy teacher?

- Don't encourage him by flirting back!
- If the attention is unwelcome and you feel like he's harassing you, mention it to another trusted teacher in the same department. Hopefully, if they have a quiet word he'll get the message.

- Make sure you've got a friend with you if you need to see him about anything outside class hours. That way you've got a witness to back you up if he starts getting creepy.
- If you feel embarrassed because he singles you out for attention then ask to move classes – or tell him directly that you don't appreciate being the teacher's pet.

Jenna's advice

The main advice I have for anyone possibly interested in a relationship with their teacher is *keep it to your-self*. There's probably no way it could work anyway –

the age difference, for one thing, is probably too great. When all your friends get boyfriends you might feel like you need to have one too and that can make you feel attracted to someone you wouldn't normally go for. But don't feel discouraged, as your time will come.

Don't build up your hopes if you think your teacher is singling you out for more attention. People will start to notice if you flirt back and hang around him. I'm not saying you shouldn't have little chats or be friends, but if things go any further and you get found out then it could ruin both your lives. **99**

Contacts

Youth Access
Tel: 01509 210420
Phone between 9 a.m. and 5 p.m. weekdays for details of your nearest Youth Counselling Service.

ChildLine
Tel: 0800 1111

Tricia Kreitman
MIZZ Agony Aunt, 27th Floor, King's Reach Tower, Stamford Street, London SE1 9LS
Unfortunately, Tricia cannot enter into personal correspondence.

"YOU DO KNOW I'M GAY... DON'T YOU?"

Photograph posed by model

"I thought, 'No, I can't be gay' and put it out of my mind."

Fay is 18 and came to terms with the fact that she is lesbian two years ago but the problem since then has been telling family and friends. She has shared her story to try to help other teenagers who might be about to drop the bombshell too ...

> "I tried to date a few boys and realized my heart wasn't really in it."

Five years ago when I was thirteen I suddenly started to think about why I had never been interested in boys, but I thought 'No, I can't be gay' and put it all out of my mind. I always had this idea in my head that it only happened to some strange breed of people out there and I could never be one of them. I wasn't against homosexuality but I still tried to date a few boys before I realized my heart wasn't really in it.

I don't know what would have happened if I had told my parents about my doubts. We were very distant and just didn't have the sort of relationship where I would have talked about fancying people, male or female. I know my mum expected me to get good results, go to A-level college, get into university, meet a nice man, get a nice job, have some nice Catholic children and then have a nice part-time arrangement back at work. I don't know what she would have thought if she had known what was going through my head.

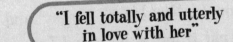

"I fell totally and utterly in love with her"

I did live up to some of the expectations, at least, and went to do three A levels when I was sixteen. I met Katy in one of my classes and somehow we got talking because we had quite a few things in common. I fell totally and utterly in love with her although at first I couldn't believe what was happening to me.

We had the same taste in books, clothes, everything and we got on so well, I couldn't believe it. I was always thinking about Katy outside college and would think, 'She's really pretty – I never noticed that before.' Then it hit me suddenly that I was actually falling in love. We had a bond I had never had with anyone else before and the way she was with me was so inspiring. She was always full of energy and always doing new things and there was also a definite physical attraction there too that I had never felt before. We used to sit and talk for hours about our problems and I could tell Katy things I could never have told anyone else. She understood me, but the one thing she didn't know was that I was gay and that I would have liked to be more than friends.

I wanted to tell her how I felt but I was scared it would be a disaster. It wasn't like I was telling a *boy* that I fancied him. I wanted to keep Katy's friendship and wouldn't have been able to bear it if she had turned round and told me I was disgusting for the way I felt. That would have made me feel totally small and worthless and I couldn't have handled it.

> "I realized people were actually scared of me"

In fact, I was too scared to even bring up the subject of gay people, because I thought she might have guessed what I was angling at. As it turned out, Katy wasn't actually the first person I told. I blurted out the truth to another mate one day and she immediately said, 'Oh no, you don't fancy me, do you?' I had to assure her I didn't. Then when the next friend I told said exactly the same thing I realized people were actually scared of me and would back off when I told them the truth. It really upset me because they were mates I had known for a long time, but once I told them the truth about being lesbian they were a bit more cool with me and I didn't see either of them as often as I used to.

In the end I didn't actually tell Katy that I was attracted to her and in love with her. All I did was tell her that I was gay and that was enough to effectively end our friendship. She jumped out of her chair and I almost laughed when she said 'You don't fancy me, do you?' just like the others. Of course, I lied and told her not to be so stupid. Katy didn't believe me, she kept saying that I couldn't be gay because I had been out with a few boys before. I said, yes, but only because of peer pressure and that quite a few lesbians have straight relationships. She just stormed out and left me sitting there.

I was in tears because I knew it was over but I was very angry as well because I thought that she, of all people, might have understood me. I didn't dare hope for a relationship with her because deep down I knew she was 100% straight, but she might have at least *understood*. When I got home that night I sat in my room thinking and I knew that she was not the person I thought she was. All that time I thought she was quite easygoing and open-minded, and she wasn't at all. I was so disappointed.

I went back to being alone again and felt quite lonely and isolated. It was about that time I decided that I couldn't keep the truth inside any longer. It was time to tell my mum. (I'd almost done it before but had backed out because of plain fear.) I felt a sudden sense of determination, so I grabbed my camera and went into the living room, where Mum was sitting reading the paper. I sat in the corner and came out with it. I said, 'Mum, you do know I'm gay, don't you?' and as she looked up, I took a picture. I'll always keep that photo – she's got her hands to her head and the paper has gone limp in her lap. I mean, she was so shocked she didn't even realize there had been a flash and I'd taken the shot. She just said, 'Oh, I didn't know that' and went back to the paper as if nothing had happened. It was as though she didn't like the news so she didn't hear it.

I walked straight out of the room and went to where my dad was and told him, but he hardly reacted and said that he already knew. I had actually hinted to him a few months before so it didn't come as a total surprise. I couldn't believe it, but I was relieved that he hadn't brought the subject up first. Dad's concern was that I was happy about being gay, and I could tell him I was. Although Mum ignored the news because she couldn't handle it, I could feel nothing but relief that I had told them both. It was the best thing to do, definitely.

> "The best thing of all now is that I can be honest"

Just after I told my parents I was sitting in the college refectory when I was introduced to my present girlfriend, Joanna. Straight away, I thought 'She's queer' and the next thing I thought was 'My God, she's quite nice too!' I think it was love at first sight and after four months we started living together. We are actually engaged now – I have a ring – and hope to go through some sort of marriage ceremony in the next few years. It was love at first sight with Joanna and I am happier now than I have ever been. We go around with a group of young lesbians in our area and we all get on really well. But the best thing of all now is that I can be honest about myself and that the real me is out in the open.

Homosexuality: Are you sussed?

There are so many rumours about gay people that it can be hard to know what to think. But if we all live together, we should try to understand more about our sexuality. Answer true or false to the following points and find out how many untruths about gay people you believe.

1. Gay people are just born that way and don't have a choice about the way they are.
2. Gay people can never have children.
3. Your friends will hate you if you tell them you're gay.
4. It's legal to have a lesbian relationship at any age.
5. Gay people are more promiscuous than straight people.
6. Lesbians only want to be your mate if they fancy you in the first place.
7. No one is 100% straight anyway.
8. It's trendy to be gay.
9. You can tell someone is gay just by looking at them.
10. You will never get a good job if you tell people you are gay.

Answers

1. Who knows?!

People still argue about whether homosexuality is something inbuilt, or whether gays make the choice to be attracted to people of the same sex. Everyone's experience of discovering their own sexuality is very different, with some saying that they knew from early childhood they were homosexual. Other people might not even realize until the opportunity of a gay relationship arises.

2. False
Gay people can, and do, have children all the time, either by adoption, artificial insemination or through an arrangement between male and female friends.

3. False
Although it is possible that some people will react badly if you tell them about your homosexuality, you can only hope that your best friends will stand by you. They may be shocked or annoyed that you didn't have the confidence to tell them before, but after the initial surprise you can try to make sure that the basic friendship is still as strong.

4. True
The law makes no mention of lesbian sex, so there is nothing illegal about it and no age of consent either. (Although if an older woman has sex with a young girl she could be guilty of sexual abuse.) Gay men must be 18 before they can legally have sex.

5. False
If you look at the population as a whole, there are always going to be people who like to have sex and those who would rather have a cup of tea and a good book instead. The gay community is just the same – of course there are very promiscuous people with lots of lovers, but there are others who can take it or leave it!

6. False
As we read in Fay's story, it's natural to think "She fancies me!" when a mate comes out to you. Why else would she bother to tell you? Well, it could just be that all she needs from you is help and support rather than a relationship. If straight girls can have boys who are mates, what's to stop lesbians having girls as friends too?

7. True
It's believed that our sexuality is never totally straight or gay, and we could think of it in terms of a spectrum with "totally gay" at one end and "totally straight" at the other. There are so many places in between for people who like lovers of both sexes, perhaps only fantasize about the same sex, and those who actually find homosexuality the biggest turn-off ever. Again, it's up to us because no two sexualities are the same!

8. False
Most people find that recognizing the fact that they are gay is one of the biggest things to happen in their lives and is certainly not something they have done to follow a trend.

9. False
There's absolutely no way of telling if someone is gay, so it's wrong to make assumptions about someone's sex life by just looking at them. Some people like to make it known that they are gay and that's where your familiar image of the gay man or lesbian may come from.

10. False
There are certain professions where it might not be the done thing to make it public knowledge that you are gay. People in the armed forces are forbidden to

have homosexual relationships and may be expelled if they are proven to be gay. People in all walks of life are gay, even though they may not choose to make their private life public knowledge.

Advice

If you think you are gay

Be sure of yourself
If you feel confused about your sexuality or haven't quite made up your mind if you like boys, girls or both, then it might be an idea to talk to someone about your mixed emotions. Ring Gay Switchboard for a chat (see 'Contacts', page 91). You may have a crush on another girl or have had fantasies about a relationship with someone of the same sex, but that doesn't mean you are definitely gay for the rest of your life. Talk it out with someone who knows more on the subject.

Come out to yourself first
It's important that you come to terms with the fact that you are gay before you decide to tell anyone else all about it, and that means you'll have to look at your feelings closely. How will it affect your life, your family, your friends, your future? You can't hide what you are, but you can at least prepare yourself for other people's reactions and know what's what before you make the big announcement.

Be self-assured
Don't let anyone tell you about your own sexuality, because it's a really personal thing and something

only you can understand! So when people say that you might grow out of it they could be right, but that's totally up to you. If you are gay, then it's your choice and you shouldn't have to tailor your sexuality to what other people want.

Prepare for your parents to be upset
There may be people who are obviously going to take the news badly. For parents, the fact that you are gay has lots of implications. You may decide not to have children, and the only wedding you're likely to have is a gay ceremony. That means your parents' future might not be what they expected and that can be a shock.

Choose your moment to break the news
You might never find the right moment to tell the people who matter to you that you're gay. However, you have to think about how they might take the news. Try to keep your conversation private, so you can have the chance to talk honestly and get emotional if you want to.

Socialize
If you get out and about and meet other young people in your situation then you'll know you're not alone with the problems and dilemmas faced by young lesbians. Ask at the local library for information, or ring Gay Switchboard and ask if they know of any groups near by.

Fay's advice
If you think you might be gay I would advise you to talk to a school or college counsellor or someone outside the immediate situation. Even if you are totally

happy about being gay it can get really confusing because you might start to doubt what you feel. Also, phone up a helpline and check for groups in your area, because that way you´il get to know other young lesbians and won't feel so alone. You might be surprised because you may know some of the people there already! Then it's a good idea to start hinting to parents, maybe to test the waters a bit. I might have made a mistake with my mum, telling her I was gay as a sort of statement. I should have opened the subject more as a discussion point and told her, 'I think I *might* be gay.' As for telling someone you are attracted to, if it's a friend then you definitely need to take things quite gently because you don't know what their feelings are. I hate to say this, but you must be prepared to be hurt too. It's probably never going to be easy to tell other people but it's better than pretending to be something you are not.

91

Contacts

London Lesbian and Gay Switchboard
Tel: 0171 837 7324 (24-hour national service)
Advice and counselling for gay people on all matters.

Families and Friends of Lesbians and Gays (FFLAG)
PO Box 153, Manchester M60 ILP
Provide advice and support on coming out to family and friends, as well as help for parents of gay young people.

London Lesbian Line
Tel: 0171 251 6911
Advice for lesbians.

"WE'VE MOVED TO THE OTHER SIDE OF THE WORLD!"

Photograph posed by model

"I dreaded having to start yet another school"

Linda, 15, had just settled in to her new school with difficulty when her stepfather got a new job in southern Africa. Here's how she coped with yet another scary new start ...

During the summer, just before going into fourth form, I dyed my hair blond from my natural dark brown colour. It was against school rules, so I was expelled and had to move to another school nearby. I couldn't believe it – I was going to have to leave all my friends behind and start again. I was terrified!

"I was miserable because I missed all my old mates and I hated the new place"

As I feared, I found it quite difficult to settle when I got there because it seemed to me that everyone had formed groups already and the place was so massive that it was easy to get lost. Everyone seemed to stay away from me because I was the new girl. Eventually I did meet a few people that I could walk to and from school with but I always felt like I was tagging along. I was miserable because I missed my old mates and I hated the new place. If someone had told me I was about to move and go through it all again I would have screamed!

But then, after a month, I came home one day and Mum said she wanted to talk to me about something. She said that my stepdad John, who's an architect, was taking a new job. I was pleased, but she explained there was a catch, that the contract was for two years in a country called Lesotho, in southern Africa. I was shocked at first and when we talked about it I was really quite scared. I dreaded having to start at yet another school and go through all the problems of fitting in all over again, and it was on the other side of the world! I even decided that I couldn't go and that I was moving in with my dad and my stepmum, and my stepbrothers and stepsisters. But even after a few days I knew it was never going to work out because my dad and stepmother's rules were so different to my mum's and I wouldn't have as much freedom – or as much pocket money.

> "It would be silly to pass up such an amazing opportunity to live in another country"

I didn't know whether to go, but when I talked to my best friend Cara, she told me that no one wanted me to, but it would be silly to pass up such an amazing opportunity to live in another country. She advised me to think of it as a long holiday and said we'd always be friends no matter what. So, I made my mind up to go and set to work because Mum and I only had about three weeks to get the stuff packed up and move over there. John had already gone out there to find a place to live.

Before I left I got fifteen friends from my old school together and Mum let us have the house to ourselves for a pyjama party. When they left next morning there were a few tears, but I was the only one who didn't get upset. Maybe I was too excited for that.

I don't think what was happening actually sank in until we landed in Lesotho. John came to pick us up, and although it was February, the heat almost knocked me over – it was 43 degrees.

> "I was stunned at the poverty; there were people living in shacks"

We drove through some suburbs towards the town and I was stunned at the poverty; people were living in shacks. The centre of the capital city was tiny and I was amazed to see that there were no pavements and only a couple of shops in the main street. There was only tinned food to eat and luxuries cost about three times what they did at home.

I started international school the same week, and on my first day met the headmaster, and was shown around. It was tiny in comparison to the old place as there were less than thirty pupils in my year. I felt really nervous about meeting people, but everyone was very friendly. I was determined not to make the mistakes I'd made at the last place, but I didn't get off to a very good start after all ...

On my first day I was told to sit in the library to do an assessment test. A succession of other pupils sneaked in to have a look at me and I found out later they were having a competition to guess what nationality I was. I didn't take much notice of them, but one boy I spied was very good looking. Then I was invited to a party on the first weekend after I had arrived and I got talking to the same boy, Craig. He told me he'd won the bet because he guessed I was English. I ended up getting off with him, but no one had told me that he was actually going out with Alicia, the most popular girl in the school! For a while I thought I had completely blown it because lots of people told me it was really nasty of me. I got an instant reputation but in the end Alicia forgave me quite quickly. I think she realized what a flirt he was.

Then I made a really nice friend, Lucy, who's from Dublin. I don't remember this, but she says she came up to me in class and introduced herself and I said, 'I'm Linda, I'm English' and she said I sounded really pompous. But we were in loads of classes together and became great friends – she reminds me of Cara so much and we're getting on really well.

I'm now doing international GCSEs and since that first hiccup I've settled in well and I'm enjoying my new life. I do get homesick sometimes. Mum and I sit and cry watching *Inspector Morse* because England looks so nice. Cara and I write a lot and she always gives me the gossip from home and passes on messages from other people I used to know. It's lovely that people remember me.

Living in Lesotho really changed the way I looked at the world and made me appreciate simple things in life, like walking down the street alone. It's too dangerous here and I know some of the other people at my school have guns in their lockers. There's the poverty too. I mean, you go to school and see pictures of starving Africans in your books, but you can shut them and try to think about something else. Out here, I've lived amongst it and I've seen hungry people living on the streets all around me. That's changed me.

> "I'm trying not to think about leaving my friends in Lesotho behind"

I'm going to go back to England this year and start college, and this time I'll be able to stay with my dad and stepfamily. Things like pocket money and staying up late seem petty when you've seen people starving and I think my new life has changed my priorities. I know I'll settle quickly back home, but I'm trying not to think about leaving my mates in Lesotho behind. I do know I won't be nervous about starting college and making new friends there. I've made a new life for myself on the other side of the world and feel that if I can do that, I can do anything!

Could you cope with a move?

Linda has coped twice with making new friends and starting new schools. But could you cope just as well if you were in her shoes and forced to make a fresh start? Try our quiz and find out how easy it would be for you to fit in ...

1. If your mum told you the family was to move abroad, would you feel ...
a Excited.
b Frightened.

2. When it came time to say goodbye to all your old friends how would you feel?
a Determined to stay in touch, no matter what.
b Sad to be losing such a good bunch of friends.

3. If other pupils ignored you on your first day at school you'd probably ...
a Have to make even more effort to make friends.
b Feel even more awkward and embarrassed about fitting in.

4. If you found out that, like Linda, you'd snogged someone else's boyfriend, you'd ...
a Apologize for the mistake and try to explain that you had no idea he was 'taken'.
b Refuse to take the blame – someone should have told you what was what before this happened.

5. Writing to your old school friends is something that ...
a You could really get into and enjoy.
b You'd like to do, but you'd probably never get round to it.

6. The best way for you to make new friends at a new school is …
a Smile and make the effort to talk to everyone.
b Smile and make the effort to talk to people you like the look of.

How did you score?

If you answered mostly a
You'll make the effort to make mates and are a naturally friendly person, so you wouldn't have too much trouble fitting in anywhere. Of course, it all comes down to luck. You might meet your new best friend on your very first day, or it might take quite a while to fit in with the others or find the sort of crowd you feel comfortable with. But any sort of friend is a start, and once you get in with one person it's amazing how many others you will be introduced to.
Tip from Linda: "Smile! It's amazing how many people will talk to you if you look friendly!"

If you answered mostly b
You expect other people to make moves to become your friend, so try not to give off unfriendly vibes to people you don't think are your type. It's not that you don't want to make mates or fit in the new place, just that your natural defences are up because you're scared! Being the new girl at school is never going to be easy, but if you try to relax and seem friendly to everyone from the dinner ladies to the head, you might soon become as popular as you were in the old place!
Tip from Linda: "It might take longer than you expected to make a really good friend, but it will happen eventually."

Advice

Moving away?

Try not to blame your parents

Sometimes the decision is taken out of your hands and it's announced that your life is going to be changed and that the move is definite, whether you like it or not. It seems hard to believe, but your parents are doing it for the good of the family as a whole. They have probably agonized over the decision and are hoping you will back them in it and look forward to your new life. It's natural to put up a fight, but think about the practical reasons they must have for wanting these changes. Can you blame them for wanting to make the move?

Don't think your old friends will desert you

Your old mates may not be in touch every day, it's true, but it's doubtful that moving away is going to see the end of your friendship. You might even find that your popularity will soar when your mates think of those holidays, visiting you at the new place! Think positive – if you are good mates, then a few miles won't change a thing. Reunions will be really special, and there's always the Royal Mail!

It doesn't take a lot to make new mates

So you think you're going to be a friendless hermit when you get to the new place? No way, not if you take the right sort of action. No matter how daunting that new school seems, we guarantee there's someone there who could be just as good a friend to you as anyone in the class you left behind. Think back to when you started secondary school or joined a new club, and remember the people you've got to know since then. It's easy – you can do it! You just have to make sure you appear friendly because no one will approach you if you look like you don't want to know. It might take a while to get in with your ideal crowd, but you will get there in the end!

Don't mope in your new home
The temptation is to stay at home and feel a bit sorry for yourself. But don't look to the past and everything you've left behind – if those mates are important to you they'll be there for ever! Making new friends and getting to know the area should be your top priority now, so find out about school groups you can join or check out the library to find out more about what's going on around you.

Be truthful about the new you
Moving house is the ideal chance to reinvent yourself! You may not have a history at the new place, so people don't know that you used to have terrible spots, or that you've been stood up more than anyone else at your old school. What you shouldn't do is tell lies to impress, because there's nothing surer than that your new mate's cousin's driving instructor's aunty knows the truth about you, and it will all get out in the end! So, it's fair to be selective about what you want to tell people, but adding to the truth will only get you into trouble.

If you are going abroad . . .
Then, like Linda, you have a bit more to acclimatize to than someone who's moving to the next town! You

might be fazed by the change in culture and people, but talking to others your own age is also the best way to learn a new language or find out more about what your town has to offer, so don't be shy. You might be the most popular addition the school has had in ages just because you're a bit of a foreign novelty!

Linda's advice

Don't give up trying to make friends, and if it doesn't happen straight away then don't let it get you down. Always try to think positive and don't dwell too much on everything you have left behind. Just try to tell yourself that things will get better if it doesn't work out at first. I've found the best way to make friends is to appear to be happy and approachable. I know it sounds strange, but after I'd settled in a couple of people told me that when I started I didn't look too friendly. If you want to meet new people then you really have to act like you want to.

When you leave your old friends behind it's a good idea to have a leaving get-together like I did because it helps you remember the people you care about. If you are good enough mates then distance can help strengthen your friendship. Oh, and another bit of advice ... make sure you know who's going out with who before you get off with anyone at a party!

Contacts

YMCA
Tel: 0181 520 5599
If you're moving to another area of Britain look in the phone book for the number of a local YMCA (Young Men's Christian Association), or ring the above

national number for details. They've got loads of activities you can get involved in and it's a great way to meet new people. PS: You don't have to be young man or a Christian, despite the name of the organization!

Youth Clubs UK
11 St Bride Street, London EC4A 4AS
Tel: 0171 353 2366
Write or ring for details of a youth club near you.

103

"I WON'T LET PERIODS RUIN MY LIFE"

Photograph posed by model

"One day I'd be crying, the next I'd be asking if anyone had a tampon"

Julia, 16, from Cumbria, always accepted her violent mood swings and depression as part of her personality. It wasn't until her mum realized the worst days came just before Julia's period that a solution to her problem was in sight ...

> **"I took it for granted it was my personality at fault"**

I always thought that there were cheerful people in this world and those who feel bad most of the time and I happened to be one of the sad, crappy, worth-

less types. I took it for granted that the terrible mood swings I had were because my personality was at fault and I would never be truly happy. It's like if you go for a night out and something spoils your fun, you'll only remember what upset you, not the fun you might have had up until that point. With me, the good times in my life didn't register. So even though I was having a couple of weeks out of the month that were OK, I didn't think about them because I spent the rest of the time acting like what a mate of mine described as 'psycho bitch from hell'.

> "I started to get so ratty and irritable that I would cry at absolutely anything"

I was 13 when my periods started and the problems came almost right away. I started to get so ratty and irritable that I would cry at absolutely anything. I was convinced everyone hated me and was paranoid that even my friends were against me. For example, I was sitting in a classroom with some mates once and they were talking about a T-shirt they had seen in the shops that they'd thought was a really disgusting colour. Somehow I got it into my head that they were having a go at me because I happened to have a skirt in a similar shade. I thought they were secretly trying to tell me that I had terrible taste in clothes.

> "I'd be in bed by eight every night, depressed and tired out"

I also became convinced that I was really fat, ugly and horrible and no one was ever going to want to go out with me because I was so awful. Of course I always got spots before my period too. And I wouldn't help myself because I would come home from school and spend the hour before Mum came home beating up my sister for doing something as innocent as leaving a light switch on. Either that or eating. In a typical teatime I'd have an iced bun, a couple of slices of toast and a bowl of cornflakes and then a whole tub of ice cream. I was completely down on myself and used to think, 'You can't even control your eating habits. You're a complete failure.' Then I'd be in bed by eight every night, depressed and tired out.

People were always asking me if there was anything the matter, but I'd get narky and tell them to leave me alone because I was fine. No wonder people thought I was a bit weird and moody, when I'd be laughing and joking a couple of weeks later like I didn't have a care in the world.

One day at school was particularly bad and I spent almost half the day crying in the toilets over nothing in particular. Of course, when I got to one class I was almost half an hour late and the teacher demanded to know where I had been. I was trying my best to hold it together, but I ran off to the toilet and shut myself in a cubicle for the rest of the day. When people came to ask what was the matter I'd tell them to go away because I thought they were just pretending to be concerned and didn't care at all. What was the matter with me?

One day I would be crying in the classroom and the next I'd be asking if anyone had a tampon, and it began to click that there might be a link there. Plus, one of my school friends actually rang my mum to ask if there was anything wrong and to draw her attention to the fact that I was acting very strangely. I think

Mum always had an inkling that my periods were bad, because she'd had a tough time too when she was younger, so she decided to keep a closer eye on me. I had no idea she was doing it, but she started to keep a sort of diary of all my symptoms. After only a couple of months she noticed that everything seemed to be so much worse for me (both mentally and physically) in the couple of weeks before my period started. She got the address of a group called PMS Help who try to help women with Pre-Menstrual Syndrome and got some leaflets back from them to explain what it was all about. When she read them it seemed there was no doubt about it, all my symptoms were exactly as they described them.

At first Mum showed me the chart she'd kept for me and tried to explain, but I was in one of my bad weeks and told her not to be stupid and to stop checking up on me all the time. I thought she was talking rubbish, but when she left the PMS info lying around I agreed to try the diet outlined in one of the leaflets, which meant I would be eating a starchy snack every three hours or so instead of the usual breakfast, lunch and dinner. In place of two slices of toast in the morning I would have one, but then have a sandwich at break. At lunchtime I'd have the other half of the sandwich and when I got home, a packet of crisps. It all seemed to fit in with my routine so well, because I could have a meal as normal in the evening, but leave afters until a couple of hours later. At first it did seem like I was eating more than ever, but in reality I was spreading the same amount of food out through the whole day. Because I was keeping my body fuelled, I wasn't getting those cravings that used to have me reaching for the biscuit tin.

> ## "The diet made a difference immediately. Everything seemed to be so much easier"

The diet made a difference immediately. Everything seemed to be easier, and suddenly my period would be over for another month and I'd still be in a good mood. The change was unbelievable, and other people noticed too.

I've been on this diet for two years now and I have come to depend upon it. I am so much happier at school and with my friends, but I never go anywhere without a packet of biscuits or something to keep me going if I'm delayed and can't eat at the normal times. It can get embarrassing sometimes, like once when I was at a friend's for dinner and I had to ask her mum if I could please have some biscuits. She said, 'Dinner's only going to be in an hour', so I had to explain that I had to eat right then or my PMS might flare up. And it does, I've missed mealtimes before and could feel the symptoms creeping back.

Some friends at school are very interested in why I have to eat so frequently, but most see it as some sort of joke and don't realize how serious it is for me. They make jokes about it being 'that time of the month' but PMS really does wreck people's lives. People who didn't know me before don't realize what I used to be like. I'm a completely different, happier person now. I can't believe food can make so much difference to my life.

I've since heard of one girl whose parents were threatening to put her into care because of her violent mood swings, but it was all down to PMS. Just changing her diet has helped her too, so no one can tell me that this is a problem to be suffered in silence.

I'm only glad my mum knew how to help me and together we found a solution – God knows what my life would have been like otherwise. **"**

Test your body knowledge

For some girls, periods are a minor inconvenience once a month. But for others they can rule, or even ruin, their lives. Try our checklist quiz and find out how much of a curse your periods really are ...

Tick the statements that apply to you and your body.

Before and during my period ...

1. I can burst into tears when confronted with minor problems.

2. I feel so fat and bloated!

3. I'm always getting more spots.

4. I feel myself getting angry for no reason.

5. I get cravings for certain foods.

6. I get terrible cramp in my stomach.

7. I can get pains in my back.

8. I can't even think about exercising.

Ticked any of the above? Check out our advice points and find out how to beat your period blues ...

1. Problem: Getting emotional
Reason: At this time of the month you are on an emotional roller coaster because the levels of hormones in your body are rising and falling. This could mean anything from being on top of the world to feeling like you can't go on.
Solution: Cut junk food, caffeine and sugar out of your diet and switch to mineral water instead of fizzy drinks. Then think about following the starchy 'snack' type of meals we've outlined below in our advice section.

2. Problem: Bloatedness
Reason: Your body tends to retain water when your period is due, and you may get a shock when you try on your tightest jeans. Your breasts may also feel swollen and tender for the same reason.
Solution: Cut salt out of your diet. If you need more help ask your GP about diuretic pills, which help stop water retention.

3. Problem: Spots
Reason: It's those hormones again! Your skin tends to get slightly more greasy before your period starts.
Solution: Make sure you keep your skin scrupulously clean at all times of the month, and *don't pick* because it could spread infection. Why not give yourself a full facial when you're feeling at your pre-menstrual worst? A little pampering might be what you need at this time of the month!

4. Problem: Anger
Reason: Just as some girls get depressed and despondent, others find they easily lose their temper; changing hormone levels are, again, to blame.
Solution: Try our tips for beating PMS and don't be

ashamed of explaining what the problem is to other people. Your parents, mates and boyfriend can learn to look for those PMS signs and know now is not the time to wind you up!

5. Problem: Food cravings
Reason: Your blood sugar levels may be falling before your period, so cravings are your body's way of making sure you take in the food necessary for your metabolism to stay steady.
Solution: Try a piece of fruit rather than a bar of chocolate! The healthier the food you eat is, the more chance you have of combating pre-menstrual problems without resorting to medicines.

6. Problem: Stomach cramps
Reason: Your womb contracts in order to help dispel the matter shed every time you have a period.
Solution: Try walking about a bit, or some gentle stretching exercises; or it may feel better to have a long bath or place a hot water bottle on your stomach. If none of these solutions work, try a painkiller. There are some on the market specifically designed for the relief of period pain.

7. Problem: Back pain
Reason: The womb isn't right at the front of your body, like you might think. Sometimes contractions or period pain may feel closer to the small of your back than your stomach.
Solution: As for stomach cramps, but try sitting up with a hot water bottle tucked into the small of your back.

8. Problem: Lethargy
Reason: The depressive symptoms of PMS may make

you flake out, or it could be because you're having to cope with aches and pains while getting on with your life.

Solution: You'll probably find that a bit of exercise will help when you're having period pain too, and could also sort out those stomach cramps when your period finally arrives. You can take any sort of exercise you enjoy doing – including swimming.

Advice

What is Pre-Menstrual Syndrome?
Doctors have discovered that some women suffer from this illness just before they have their periods. The symptoms are never apparent more than fourteen days before their period starts and usually disappear for at least seven days once they have started to menstruate.

What are the signs?
The symptoms vary, but always come back every time a period is due. Each woman has to cope with a combination of complaints as it's very rare to suffer from only one. There are said to be more than 150 different symptoms, and they can be physical (backache, sore breasts, bloatedness, migraine, asthma attacks, etc.) or mental (depression, tension and tiredness, amongst others).

How do you know if you've got PMS?
If you feel that you could be experiencing mood swings, depression or physical symptoms like the ones listed above then the best thing to do is to keep a sort of diary of your moods and feelings. This will help you pinpoint the days you feel bad and link them

to when your period starts and ends. Try to keep this diary for at least three months, and if you begin to notice a pattern then it's time to act to beat PMS!

How can PMS be treated?

If you think you might have some of the symptoms of PMS then the first thing to do is to look at what you eat – and when you eat it. Doctors have discovered that eating small portions of starchy foods every three hours helps a lot, no matter what the time of the month. Recommended foods contain flour, rice, oats, potato, maize or rye; so menus including pasta, bread, baked potatoes or corn on the cob will do the trick. You may also find that eating at least four portions of fruit or veg every day can help. It's also important that you eat within one hour of waking up and one of hour of going to bed at night. Dividing your meals into six or seven healthy snacks may seem strange when you're used to eating breakfast, lunch and dinner, but this method really can work and is worth trying.

If diet doesn't work . . .

If you try the special diet and don't seem to have made any improvement when you check out your three-month diary, then it might be time to look for more help. Take your menstrual charts along to show your GP and he or she should be able to prescribe a drug (progesterone) to help if more natural treatment has failed.

Julia's advice

Keep a chart, for starters. And if you think your friend, sister or whoever has a problem with PMS you can do it for them like my mum did for me. But don't

accost them with the evidence when they're having a bad day!

   PMS may have become a bit of a joke but I know how bad it can be, so please act. Your complaints will get much better and you'll feel as though you're in control of your body again. So many girls I know will go and have a fight with someone or get upset and simply blame 'that time of the month' but you have to ask yourself if it's worth it. It's so easy to help yourself; and to help your family and friends, because they're suffering too, having to cope with your moods.

Contacts

PMS Help
PO Box 83, Hereford HR4 8YQ
Some excellent leaflets are available at £1 each from the above address – please include a stamped addressed envelope. Titles include *Too Young For PMS?*, which is a guide for teenage girls on how to help themselves and their friends.

Pre-Menstrual Syndrome Society
PO Box 102, London SE1 9ES

"JEALOUSY RUINED OUR FRIENDSHIP!"

Photograph posed by model

"I was in awe of Sharon at first, but then that turned into real resentment ..."

15-year-old Jayne, from Essex, never had much confidence in herself or her looks. When she made friends with the prettiest, richest girl in school, jealousy eventually tore the friendship apart ...

When I first met Sharon she was the new girl at school and I got the job of showing her round. I'm quite shy and I don't have much confidence, but she was very outgoing and funny. She said she was feeling really nervous about her first day. I didn't think my friends Emma and Lynette would mind if she joined us so I told her where to meet us at break. I couldn't believe I had made a new friend.

We asked Sharon all about herself and by the way she mentioned places she'd been on holiday and the area she'd moved to, I quickly realized that her family had a lot of money. I had never heard of the car business her dad owned, but when I mentioned it to my mum she said Sharon's dad was probably worth millions! My mum and dad are both teachers, so we're not exactly on the breadline but just not in her family's league. When I saw Sharon's house for the first time I told her it was like a mansion and she laughed and said, 'You should have seen the last place.' I was in awe of her at first, and it felt awful to go back to our semi afterwards.

> "Even after a few weeks,
> I secretly hated her at times"

Sharon and I spent all our time together but it bugged me that we weren't on equal terms and even after a few weeks, I secretly hated her at times. She was always charming with other people but with me she was bossy and quite domineering. She'd say things like, 'Iron that shirt for me, Jayne' and I would do it because I didn't want to lose her. It was great, the way she lent me her expensive clothes and how her parents would take us to restaurants on Saturday nights. I wanted it all for myself, but at the time I thought the next best thing was to have a mate who had it instead.

> "Instead of running to tell her someone
> fancied her I never said a word"

Everyone knew we were best friends, but my resentment grew even stronger when rumours started going round that loads of boys in sixth form fancied Sharon. My cousin Scott went to our school and told me every bloke he knew would like to get their hands on her. I did know she was popular but it hurt because no one would ever have said that about me. Instead of rushing to tell her someone fancied her I never said a word, but I suppose she eventually found out from someone else. I even said to Scott that if boys knew what Sharon was really like then they would be surprised because she was a bitch and a spoiled little princess. He said he'd always thought we were best mates, so I felt a twinge of guilt admitting we still were.

Once, I went past the common room and she was in there talking to Mark, a sixth year boy I'd liked for ages the previous summer. He was saying, 'That's a fake, right?' as he looked at her watch. Sharon pretended to be totally affronted when he said, 'It must be, those cost a grand at least.' She smiled and said her birthday presents got better every year and she was getting a Beetle when she was 17. I couldn't bear it. I would have done anything to be her at that moment. She was so pleased with herself.

> "I wasn't pleased about the amount of attention she was getting"

Once, her mum dropped her off at the school after the dentist's and we could see her get out of the car from our chemistry lab. Or we wouldn't if someone hadn't shouted, 'Check Sharon's mum out!' and everyone stared out of the window, even the teacher!

I pretended nothing had happened but I wasn't pleased for her at all, or about the amount of attention she was getting. I felt terrible the next day when Mark came over to ask if it was true her mum had a new Merc. I went off and cried in the toilets because I felt so awful about the attention she was getting.

The more adoration Sharon got from the lads or from other girls, the worse I felt. It could have been her shoes, or her hair, or how long her eyelashes were or how amazingly funny she was and I hated her more with every compliment she got. I felt insecure about everything and resented my mum if she wouldn't give me money for new clothes or shoes. I hated having to buy stuff from Miss Selfridge like everyone else. It was all starting to cause fights at home because Mum said Sharon was a bad influence on me and I wasn't going to get spoiled like she was. I never told Sharon about any of this because I didn't want her to think I couldn't have what I wanted too. It would have made me feel too low about myself to admit I was inferior.

I made a real effort for the school Christmas dance and got really dressed up, then Sharon called round for me in a Versace suit she said was her mum's. I hated her then – how could I compete with someone whose mum had better clothes than me?

Although the dance was at school, we got really drunk on the way there. By halfway through the night Sharon had to come into the toilets to get me because I was in a real state. She grabbed my chin and said, 'Look at you, you're a mess. You're showing me up.' I felt bad about myself anyway so something in me changed and I pushed her away and asked her who the hell she thought she was, snobby bitch, telling me what I should do. She looked really surprised and hurt and just kept saying 'Shut up', but I carried on shouting. The embarrassment of her talking down to me in front of everyone just killed me. I wanted her to know what it felt like. Then Mark and some of his mates came in and they were laughing and going, 'Ooh, Jayne – temper, temper.' I hated the way everyone always sided with her when they didn't know what she was really like. I went upstairs on the dancefloor and didn't talk to her or anyone else for the rest of the night. I saw people gossiping about me but I didn't care because I wanted them to hate her, and if people were talking about me they'd be telling each other what I had said to her, wouldn't they?

> "She's everything I would like to be, but I do hate her personality"

Mark was obviously annoyed, because he passed me at one point and said 'Gold-digger.' That was rich coming from him, but I was seething and went straight home without even collecting my coat. The friendship finished there, as simple as that, and although my mum's asked what happened to Sharon I don't tell her that she wouldn't want to see me. That was Christmas '94 and I have hardly spoken to her since then. I'm quite friendly with Lynette again but I still look at Sharon and feel bad – she's everything I would like to be, but I do hate her personality. I resent the way people look at the clothes, the house, the person and forgive her for anything, while I'm the butt of their jokes because of that night. I know I could only have been mates with her as long as I was because I was impressed too. Now I have to take my mum's advice and get in the real world.

Are you jealous of your best friend?

She may be one of the most important people in your life, but is she also the person most likely to make you bright green with envy? Check your jealousy rating in our quick quiz ...

1. You can't believe it when the boy you secretly fancy calls you up. But then he says he's ringing to ask if you'd put a good word in for him with your mate. Do you tell her the good news?

a Yes. As soon as he rings off you rush round to tell her she's got an admirer. You'll find someone else to fancy.

b You hint that he might be a teensy bit interested, but only if she happens to comment that she likes him too.

c There's no way you're going to tell her. You couldn't bear it if she was the one to have messed up your chances.

2. Her birthday present from her parents is a shopping spree in your favourite store. What do you do when she invites you to come along with her?

a Enjoy helping her spend the money and give her your opinion on that drop-dead sexy outfit she's set her heart on.

b Go along but only because you might be able to borrow some of the stuff she buys!

c Tell her you're busy that day. You can't possibly stand in that changing room and let her rub salt in your wounds!

122

3. The teacher reads out your friend's essay and tells everyone how creative and original she has been. Your problem is that the original idea for the story was yours. How do you feel?

a Pleased that she did justice to your brilliant idea.

b Glad for her – but you let everyone know the truth after class.

c Outraged – it's all so unfair! That's the last time you give her any help.

4. She tells you that her uncle has died and has left her a massive inheritance. What's your first reaction when you hear the news?

a All you can do is worry that she might be upset about her uncle dying.

b To go round to find out how much cash she got – you won't feel jealous until you find out what exactly a 'massive inheritance' is!

c To wonder what she did to deserve such a lucky break. What a jammy cow!

5. The dresses you and your friend are wearing to Saturday night's party are quite similar, but that's not a problem for you. But is it a problem when the school bitch comments that your friend's got a better figure than you in that sort of outfit?

a No – there are plenty of things you can do better than your mate so it doesn't bother you in the slightest.

b It's nothing you can't handle, but you make a mental note to wear something different if the competition is this hot.

c It's enough to make you want to go straight back home again because you've taken a sudden dislike to being in the same room as her.

6. You're trying to impress some extra-fanciable boys when she steps in and makes a witty comment that has them falling around laughing. What are you doing when the hilarity continues?

a Laughing along with them and feeling really pleased that you have such a funny friend.

b Showing off in an attempt to show the lads you can be just as entertaining.

c Storming off because you feel like she's trying to show you up in public.

7. It's Saturday night and although you usually go out with your friend, this week she's got a date with a boy most girls you know would kill to even talk to. What are you thinking about when you're sitting at home?

a You're hoping it works out great for her and the bloke asks if he can see her again.

b That it's about time you asked someone out so you can have a bit of excitement in your life too.

c That it's just not fair that you've been dumped for a lad she's not good enough for in the first place.

8. You go on a couple of dates with a boy and then decide you don't like him and you should stop seeing each other. How do you feel when you hear he's asked your mate out?

a Happy for them both. If she likes him then she should go for it – with your blessing.

b A bit taken aback, but you realize you'd be a hypocrite if you didn't approve. After all – you chucked *him*.

c Really envious, despite yourself. You didn't want him – but you don't want her to snog him either, thanks!

If you scored mostly a
You are the sort of girl who genuinely wants the best for a mate, and you don't get jealous when something great happens to them. You're pleased when they do well and don't feel a pang of jealousy even when they put you in the shade! You've probably known your best friend for quite a while now, and because your relationship is steady and reliable there's no danger of you feeling insecure.

If you scored mostly b
It's not that you are seething with jealousy when your best mate gets one over on you, just that you like to make sure you can get one over on her afterwards! You don't exactly let envy eat you up, but it does affect you enough to make you want to go into competition with her. Chill out a bit and be yourself – life shouldn't have to be a contest, especially not with real mates.

If you scored mostly c
You are so envious of your mate that you probably believe she is totally perfect and there's nothing about her looks or personality that you wouldn't like to emulate. But hold on, if you asked her what she envied about *you* she might come up with some surprises. You see all the good things in her, but everyone has their bad points too. Accept yours and hers together and that'll make for a far better – and more realistic – friendship.

Advice

The do's and don'ts of a good friendship

DO remember that it's not *her* fault if she's got brains, talent or the attention of that boy you fancy.

DON'T try to copy her if you're jealous of the way she looks. If she's so stunning you're just going to look like an inferior version of her, so cultivate your own style and show others you've got your own mind too.

DO tell her if she's making you jealous. If she doesn't realize she's driving you mad then she'll carry on with the same sort of behaviour. That's when things build up, you blow a gasket and this friendship could end with one massive argument.

DON'T talk to other mutual friends first if you have a problem with the way she is acting. That's only going to make things more complicated when she finds out what you have been saying about her – and believe us, she will!

DO make sure you keep in contact with other mates, because it's not always healthy to spend all your time with just one friend. If you get involved in what other people are doing too it will give you both a little more space, and the chance to appreciate each other's company when you do get together.

Jayne's advice

I realized pretty quickly that Sharon was not the sort of girl I had usually had as a friend. She was very self-assured and bossy and used her confidence to make sure she got what she wanted. I don't think we were suited to be together. If I hadn't been attracted to all the material things she had and how different her lifestyle was then I don't think we would have been mates in the first place. To anyone else in the same situation, I would tell them to look at the person, not what they've got and then decide if they are a real friend. Stick to what you know, because when I tried to compete with someone like her I was like a sad loser and that made me feel really bad about myself. My confidence has been shaken, and I didn't have much of it in the first place really. Friendship shouldn't be some sort of competition and you should feel like you are on equal terms.

Contacts

Tricia Kreitman
MIZZ Agony Aunt, 27th Floor, King's Reach Tower, Stamford Street, London SE1 9LS
For practical advice on how to handle jealous friendships. Unfortunately, Tricia cannot enter into personal correspondence.

ChildLine
Tel: 0800 1111

Youth Access
Tel: 01509 210420

Phone between 9 a.m. and 5 p.m. weekdays for details of your nearest Youth Counselling Service.

"I WAS SEXUALLY ABUSED"

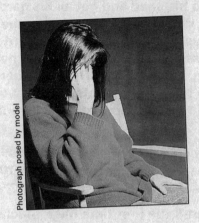

Photograph posed by model

"I thought I was dirty and evil, when he was the monster"

Sarah, from Norfolk, is nearly 18, and put up with sexual abuse from the age of 8. When she was 14 she got the courage together to tell a teacher what was happening, and now wants to share her story to encourage other sufferers to speak out ...

"My mum was great friends with our neighbours, since we moved to that house when I was 7, after my dad left. Joy and Mike were in their late fifties and their daughter had grown up and left home. Mum was always popping next door for this and that and Mike even decided to take down the garden fence to

make one big play area for me and my younger brother Andrew.

Mike always used to love playing with us and he'd let us go into his shed and get all his gardening stuff out to help with weeds or mowing the lawn. Joy would take us to the shops with her and sometimes let us tag along when she went to see their daughter who lived in the country. I never understood why Joanna didn't like her parents. Now I wonder if she hated her dad for the same reasons I would …

> **"I was far too young to understand that what he was doing to me was wrong"**

I was about 8 the first time Mike touched me – far too young to understand that what he was doing to me was wrong. I was out in the garden and I went in to their house to ask if I could have a drink. Mum was out and Mike had been asked to keep an eye on us so he poured some orange squash in a jug and asked if I wanted to put the water in myself. Then he stood behind me as I bent across the sink to reach the tap and he put his hand on my bottom, with his fingers going under the hem of my pants. I thought I must be imagining things, but when he started moving his hand about a bit I knew it wasn't a mistake. I didn't understand what he was doing but I knew I wouldn't say anything to him – I thought it would be bad manners. I thought maybe what had happened was my fault. I was making excuses for Mike already.

> **"I dreaded going to bed. When I did, Mike came in and started putting his hands all over me"**

"He said that if I told anyone they'd
take me away and put me in a home"

From then on I was always wary of Mike. I couldn't
believe it when my mum and the Bennetts booked up
to go to a holiday centre for the half-term break. The
second night of the holiday we all had dinner
together in the chalet and then Mike suggested that
Mum and Joy could go for a drink at the resort centre
and he'd stay and look after me and Andrew. He let us
stay up late to play Monopoly and I dreaded going to
bed. When I did, Mike came in and started putting his
hands all over me even though Andrew was only in
the top bunk. It was dark but I bet he could see I was
crying. He was always saying that if I told anyone
then they'd take me away and put me in a home. He
said they'd think I was making it all up, so I was so
scared I pretended I was asleep.

The abuse got worse all the time and he'd make me
touch him too. The only reason I think Mike didn't
have full sex with me was because Andrew was
there, or Mum would be downstairs or coming home
soon. I feel sorry for kids whose own fathers abuse
them because they have to live with that person 24
hours a day, every day.

I found it hard to get on with the other children at
school because I was always worrying and couldn't
enjoy myself. By the time I was 11 I was having panic
attacks, and once I went hysterical in a big shop when
I got lost for five minutes. Not a day went by when I
didn't think of Mike and worry about the next time I
was going to be alone with him.

When Mum started to work on Saturdays he'd take
us to football and touch me in the car, in broad day-

light, again with Andrew in the back. I froze every time and tried to think about other things rather than what was happening to me. I remember thinking to myself if he was prepared to take chances like that then he didn't care if he did get caught because he could say it was all my fault. It didn't occur to me just to tell someone because I thought I was the one who was in the wrong.

When I started secondary school I hardly made any friends outside the girls I had known since infants. I didn't want a boyfriend because I hated the thought of someone else trying to do things to me and I never understood when girls at school laughed and whispered about people groping each other. I didn't think it was something to laugh about at all. But gradually, the more I heard people talking about sex, the more I realized that I shouldn't have been feeling the way I did. Then I saw a male victim on a programme about abuse, saying how he wished he'd told someone earlier, and it really made me think.

I was 14 and Mike had been threatening and abusing me since I was 8 years old. He'd taken my life away and the stress and worry was going to ruin any chance I had of being happy in the future. I thought I was dirty and evil, when *he* was the monster.

One day I told my PE teacher, which was the hardest thing I ever had to do. I told her everything. She said we'd have to tell the headmistress, and when we went over there she phoned my mum at work and got her up there. She was hysterical and wanted to kill Mike, but she believed me. That was all that mattered to me.

Social workers got involved and I had to give video evidence to the police about what had happened. They also had to ask Andrew if he'd been touched, but he never had been. I went through all this like I was dreaming and when a doctor examined me for signs of abuse I switched off my mind. I was put on medication. I was scared to leave the house, even though we'd heard Joy had gone to her daughter's and Mike had disappeared. I wasn't at school for months.

> **"I told them everything but Mike said I was a liar."**

My case took ages to come to court, by which time I got myself together a bit. I was on the stand for an hour and three quarters and told them everything but Mike said I was a liar. He was found guilty of indecent assault and given two years probation and a fine. It was the worst day ever, but not as bad as having him touch me again. He didn't look at me at all during the trial and Joy wasn't there so I hope his life was ruined the way he ruined mine.

I'm nearly 18 now and I feel very bitter about what's happened. I am still seeing a counsellor who has helped me a lot and she has made me see what happened wasn't my fault. She's helped me to cope when I've been low and because my mum doesn't find it easy to talk to me about what's happened. I know Mum blames herself but the hurt has to stop now and we have to get on with our lives. I am starting college soon and I hope to get into counselling myself one day because I know how important it is to have the right sort of help. That's why I agreed to talk about this, in the hope that someone out there will read my story and realize that the only easy way to help yourself is to talk about it, and that means telling someone as soon as you can.

Advice

Who is abused?

No one deserves to be sexually abused, so never think what has happened to you is your fault. It doesn't matter how you dress, act, or relate to the person who has abused you. If you do get in contact with counsellors they will be able to help you get rid of some of the guilt and pain, but will also help you to recognize that you are a victim and in no way to blame for the abuse you have had to suffer.

Should you tell?

Even if the abuse has gone on for years and you are, in some ways, used to it, there's no way this will ever stop unless you do something. No abuser will suddenly decide to give up – often it's not something they have control over anyway. Think about it. You may not be the only one whose life is being ruined. Now if things are going to get better they might have to get worse for while and though it might be the most difficult thing you have ever done, it really is for the best. Help is out there, but you have to ask for it first.

How can you get help?

It doesn't matter if the abuse happened a long time ago. The first step to getting over it is to tell someone, and the best person to gauge who should know about it is you. In situations like this there are other people outside the family who can help give more impartial advice – and will be more likely to believe you too. You can walk in to any police station or social work office and ask for help, or you might want to tell your GP. For further advice, try ringing one of the phone helplines detailed in the contacts section.

Why does it happen?
All sorts of people are sexual abusers – male, female, rich, poor, from all walks of life. The person who sexually abuses is probably following a pattern that has been going on for years. He or she could have been abused themselves when they were younger, and it seems natural for them to do the same. They may enjoy the feeling of domination, as they are in control of the 'relationship'. The only way for the cycle to be broken is to get help from counsellors, and they often will not volunteer for that themselves. You may have to solve the problem for them by telling someone what's happening and making sure they get the help they need.

The future
Survivors of sexual abuse may have problems forming their own relationships in the future. It is difficult for them to see sexual contact as part of a loving relationship and they need help to get rid of the feelings of guilt and self-hatred that might result from the abuse. With help, there are ways of coming to terms with the past, and although the abused child or teenager will never forget what has happened to them, they can make sure it doesn't ruin their chances of finding happiness in the future.

How can you help a friend?
If they haven't confided in you
If you only suspect a friend has been sexually abused, you have to be very careful about how you tackle the

situation. It's probably best not to ask directly because their natural instinct will be to deny there's a problem. You could bring up the subject in general conversation one day, mention helplines available and let her decide when the time is right to act.

If they have confided in you
First of all, listen and support. Your friend may not be able to talk to anyone else about their experiences and will be glad of someone to share their problems with. You can offer to get some information from an advisory group on their behalf or go along with them as moral support if they decide to get help. But please remember the decision to get help should be your friend's. You can help and advise them on what you think they should do, but never force them into letting you make the decisions for them.

136

Sarah's advice

When I look back to what happened to me, I know that I should have said something the first time Mike touched me. But I was brought up to do as adults told me, and I thought no one would believe me if I told tales. It's a really serious allegation to make, I know, but as time goes on the situation will only get worse. It could go on for years and then you'll have told more lies, put up with more pain and got even more messed up. Abusers are sick people who need help as much as you do, but they will never ask for it themselves. I often wonder if Mike abused other children or his daughter, because it never came out in court. I hope by giving him a criminal record it won't happen to others too. Speak out to help yourself and others because they will go on and on destroying other people's lives too if you don't stop them.

Can you keep safe on the streets?

Sexual abuse doesn't always happen at home, and with rape figures on the increase it's more important than ever that you should know how to protect yourself. Try our quiz and pick up more tips about how you can keep safe ...

1. If you get hassled on public transport the best thing to do is ...
a Get off the bus/train as soon as possible.
b Tell the guard/driver/conductor.

2. When you're walking home alone at night ...
a Stick to the quickest route and use short cuts.
b Stay on main roads, even if it takes longer.

3. If a flasher exposes himself to you the best thing to do is ...
a Walk away as fast as you can and try to forget it happened.
b Get away to safety and report it to the police as soon as possible.

4. If you feel as though you're being followed ...
a Run if you have to, but don't look back till you get home.
b Speed up slightly and walk into a shop or pub.

5. Wearing your personal stereo at night could ...
a Make you unaware of the dangers around you.
b Make your journey go a lot quicker.

6. If you are attacked, the best thing to do is ...
a Scream, shout and make as much noise as possible.
b Keep quiet and do whatever they want.

How did you score?
Look below for our street safety tips.

1. (b) Tell the guard/driver/conductor.
If you do get off the train or bus you could be followed. Tell a member of staff, because they can phone the police or throw the person bothering you off!

2. (b) Stay on main roads, even if it takes longer.

It's not a good idea to go down dark streets or alley-ways by yourself. Always stick to main roads, where there will be plenty of people around and more street lights.

3. (b) Get away to safety and report it to the police as soon as possible.
Very often serious sexual offenders have a history of exposing themselves to strangers. Flashing isn't funny. Report what you've seen now and he may get help before it's too late.

4. (b) Speed up slightly and walk into a shop or pub.
The best thing to do is to find other people who can help. So even if it means walking up to strangers (preferably female) or asking a shop assistant for help, try to show whoever may be following you that you're not alone.

5. (a) Make you unaware of the dangers around you.
Personal stereos shouldn't be worn at night when you won't be able to hear anyone coming up behind you. You need all your senses to stay safe on the streets!

6. (a) Scream, shout and make as much noise as possible.
No one knows how they'll react until it happens to them, but making noise might frighten your attacker away or give you time to run. Better still, carry a rape alarm in your bag and use that as soon as you sense danger.

Contacts

NSPCC (National Society for the Prevention of Cruelty to Children)
Child Protection Helpline: 0800 800500

They will provide counselling for victims of sexual abuse and take action if requested.

Rape Crisis Centres
Tel: 0171 837 1600 (weekdays 6 p.m. to 10 p.m. and weekends 10 a.m. to 10 p.m.)
Confidential advice from women for women and young girls.

ChildLine
Tel: 0800 1111
Confidential counselling for young people. Remember, the number won't show on your itemized phone bill.

"MY HOME LIFE WAS HELL, SO I RAN AWAY"

Photograph posed by model

"Mum thought I'd been murdered. I'd been gone for four weeks"

Kerryanne is 16 and lives in her own bedsit in Glasgow. She first ran away from home when she was 13 years old because of her mother's alcoholism ...

My mum and I lived together in a flat and when I was a kid we seemed to get on all right. She had a few boyfriends I never got on with but apart from that we didn't disagree about much. I used to have my pals round after school because she would let us do anything we wanted, like cooking our own teas and watching certificate 18 videos.

When I started secondary school she got a job in a

factory as a machinist, which is what she'd done before she had me. She started to make a bit more money than before so sometimes went out with the girls after work on a Friday and also had parties back at our house. They were always rowdy and really drunken.

> "I actually blame him for leading Mum from being a social drinker to a full-blown alcoholic"

When she started to go out drinking during the week too I was quite pleased because I could smoke without her moaning at me. By the time I got into second year she was out most nights because she had a new boyfriend, Tam, who was a driver at her work. He was a bit of a drunk and I actually blame him for leading Mum from being a social drinker to a full-blown alcoholic. I used to get up in the mornings to try to get myself ready for school and the two of them would be lying in the lounge, still out of it from the night before. Mum started work at 8.30, so I would have to try to get her up and out as soon as I could. It was like she was the kid.

> "When I got home the next night after school Tam belted me"

> "I went up to one of the main bus stations in Glasgow and stayed there for the night"

Tam moved in for a while and my mum got pregnant and had an abortion after two months. I didn't know anything about it until after she'd gone into hospital and got rid of it. I asked where she was and Tam told me as if it wasn't important. I was really cut up, and thought about running away but I got scared so asked my friend Mandy if I could go and stay at her house that night because Mum would be coming home and I couldn't face her. I didn't leave a note about where I would be and when I got home the next night after school Tam belted me. I got my stuff and went at about one o'clock in the morning, when they had gone to bed. I went up to one of the main bus stations in Glasgow and stayed there for the night, lying on a row of seats. I remember being really scared and although I only had about two quid on me I hid it in my knickers. I didn't get any hassle, but it was the most frightening night of my life.

I spent half the money on fags anyway, so I went into school the next day because I knew I would get my free dinner. My mum came up to the head to tell him I was out of control, so I got called out of the class and into his office, where my mum was sitting there pissed. I hated her for doing that, but I went home again because she promised she would start getting her act together. We did nothing but fight because of the state she was in and the abortion. She was a mess. I even went to move her off the settee one night and she had wet herself.

Tam got a job down in Coventry, so then she was worse than ever, drinking by herself every night. I ran away again because I couldn't cope, this time to Ayr, which is near Glasgow but by the sea. It was the summertime and there were lots of people there for holidays, so I got bits of work cleaning guest houses. No one knew I was fourteen because I looked a lot older. I stayed at a campsite in a tent that one of the landladies gave me, but it was really cold because I didn't have proper sleeping bags, so I got a dog, Lady, and used to cuddle up to her for heat. Then I couldn't take hotel work any more because I had nowhere to keep her, so I was a bit stuck. I decided I'd phone to let Mum know I was OK. She was in a state, crying and calling me a selfish bitch. She told me she'd told the police and they'd been up to the flat. She was begging me to go back, because she'd been laid off and I was all she had. It was quite sad because she thought I'd been murdered. I'd been gone for four weeks.

I went back there till I was 15 but it was really hellish. I hardly ever went to school and I used to see her down at the parade of shops when I was dogging it, out in a summer dress in the middle of winter, buying cans of Special when we had no food at home.

My pals said she used to stand out by the gates, looking for me, swaying about. They were all talking about her, saying 'Kerryanne's mum's a tramp' or 'Is it true your mum's an alky?' Then there was pressure at home from looking after her and the worry of not having any money to get dinners with. She was too drunk to even go and get the dole sometimes.

I had to tell somebody about my problems because I was scared my mum was going to die if she kept on drinking. She got taken into casualty once because she collapsed out in the street, and they told her that's what would happen if she didn't sort herself out, so she did improve a bit. But Tam wormed his way back at Christmas and it doesn't look good for her future. I have joined a group called Alateen, which helps people with alcoholic parents. It's brilliant because I've met other teenagers in situations like mine and I know that I can try to help Mum, but that I have to get on with my own life as well. I eventually convinced her to go Alcoholics Anonymous and she's tried to stay off booze, but if I'm really honest I think it's a losing battle. I don't believe she'll change.

> "It's really hard to get by when you don't know anybody and have nowhere safe to stay"

I could have walked out like I had done before but that time in Ayr really taught me that I couldn't have done it for ever. There's no way you can if you care about what's happening at home. You can't leave it all behind you and it's really hard to get by when you don't know anybody and have nowhere safe to stay. I could have gone off somewhere like London and God knows what would have happened by now. I'd still be on the streets, begging maybe. Home was bad, but that's got to be worse.

I still have problems I want to walk out on, but what's the use? I've got my own bedsit now which isn't that great, but it's better than a tent! I'm working in a baker's and meeting new people. Mum and Tam seem to be all right together, since he's been getting help too, so I can only hope things get better. I want to feel safe at home and have a nice place one day with a nice man and our kids. I don't think that's too much to hope for, but a while ago I never thought it could be possible. Now I know it will if I stay and sort things out.

Can you handle problems at home?

You can choose your friends but not your family, as the saying goes. That means that home life can sometimes feel like hell on earth. But before you have

another row or even contemplate running off somewhere, try our quiz. It might help you think of new
ways to tackle your problems.

Tick the statements that best describe your home
life and your attitudes towards the other family mem-
bers you live with. Then give yourself one point for
every statement you've ticked.

☐ My family very rarely sit together to talk for more
than a few minutes.

☐ I would rather walk away from people I disagree
with than argue.

☐ I spend most of my time in my room – as far away
as possible from everyone else.

(146) ☐ I wouldn't dare disagree with my parents.

☐ I find it hard to talk to my family about problems
that don't concern them.

☐ I can't seem to tolerate my family nosing into
areas of my life that don't concern them.

☐ My opinion doesn't seem to matter, so I don't
offer it.

☐ I never get consulted about big family decisions,
like holidays.

☐ I envy the way my mates can talk to their parents.

☐ My family would be surprised if they knew the
'real me'.

If you scored...

0-3 points: Communication counts

It might seem like every discussion you have with your family turns into an argument, but at least you're still talking! Next time tempers flare, try to calm down a bit, listen to what others are saying and wait for the right time to get your message across calmly and clearly.

Tip: If things get rough and arguments are getting out of hand, try writing your feelings down, maybe in a letter to the family member your argument is with. You don't have to get nasty, but you will get the chance to state your case in peace and quiet.

4-7 points: Build on your skills

You have your ups and downs like every family, but building on the relationships you already have is the key to a harmonious home life. As you grow older you'll need different support from your parents, though they might still like to think of you as their little girl. But since you don't walk away when there's something to be discussed, you can improve your relationship if you show you can listen to your parent's side of things and prove you are ready to discuss issues like an adult.

Tip: Call for a family meeting when problems get out of hand. It can be hard to get everyone together at the same time to talk, but give them enough warning and you'll have the chance to work things out all together.

8-10 points: You don't like to talk

Sometimes your home life can be so awful that it seems that the only thing you can do to make things better is to leave it all far behind you. You're probably doing that in your own way at the moment, by shutting yourself in your room, refusing to talk or deciding it's worthless to even try sorting your life out. How long can you survive before you want to get out altogether and will have to face more practical problems, like finding somewhere to live? If you want to change your life and create a happier environment at home, you're going to have to work at it. The first step is to talk about the problems facing you and your family instead of living in denial.

Tip: If you have real difficulty talking about your unhappiness, bring in a third party to help smooth things over with your family. That could be a matter of involving another, more impartial relative, or it could mean seeking help from some of the contacts we have listed at the end of this chapter.

Advice

If you feel like running away... Stop!

DON'T think running away would be a great idea because it would teach your family a lesson. Of course they'll miss you when you're gone, but it also means there will be more problems to face in the long run if you are to sort out your differences.

DO remember there is always someone out there you can talk to about your problems. Look at the Contacts section for names of some useful groups who will be more than happy to help sort things out. They don't need to tell your family you have seen them.

DON'T do anything on the spur of the moment. After a fight, the first reaction might be for you to get as far away as possible from your problems and the people causing them, but it's really unwise to make a move without having somewhere safe to go.

DO talk to your family if your problems are caused outside the home. You may be surprised at just how much they can help – and how glad they are you confided in them.

DON'T take for granted that your problems will end as soon as your home life is left behind. OK, so things may be rough, but you still have a roof over your head at the end of the day. Try to solve your problems from home before doing anything rash.

DO ask to stay overnight at a friend's if you feel like you can't go home. But it's not a good idea to make your stay any longer, or expect to move in there unless both sets of parents give the go-ahead.

DON'T think you could run off and no one would care. No matter how convinced you are that you wouldn't be missed, we guarantee you would be!

DON'T ever run away just to teach your family a lesson – it's just too serious for that.

Where can you go?
It may be that your home situation is so intolerable that you have to get out of there as soon as possible.

But rather than pack your bags and leave without saying goodbye, why not look into the possibilities of living separately with the agreement of your family?

Relatives?
It might cause a lot less upset and bad feeling to suggest living with another relative – maybe a grandparent or aunt. But remember to organize things first because you can't expect to turn up on a doorstep with all your belongings and be taken in without warning!

Friends?
Unless they have their own place, it's a friend's parents you'll have to talk to about staying for a while. Don't be surprised if they don't want to get involved in another family's problems. They may have too much to cope with in the first place with their own kids!

Social services?
You can ask for help at any social services office, and they could arrange for you to stay with another family or in council care. They'll also try to help remedy the situation at home and work towards you going back there for good, if the problems are solved.

Another town?
It's not wise to get on a bus and head for a place you think will offer you a better future. Maybe you've got good memories of the town or believe it's easier to get work there or find a place to stay? It can be even tougher to survive when you won't have any support from people who know you, and your memories might be somewhat rose tinted. So don't hope that putting miles between you and your problems will solve them for ever. You may be introducing yourself to a whole

load of new hassles instead as it's pretty near impossible to find any sort of work when you don't have a
fixed address. Soon, you'll be getting yourself into a
no-win situation.

The streets?

Don't walk out feeling sure you'll be able to find some
sort of safe shelter for the night. You only have to look
in the doorways of shops in the big cities to see it's not
always possible to find a place to stay. Sure, you'll be
fine if you've got the cash for a cheap B&B, but the
money soon goes by keeping yourself going during
the day and if you do have to sleep rough there are
dangerous people around waiting to take advantage
of your desperate situation.

**PS: If problems at home are due to physical or sexual
abuse you must seek help as soon as possible. Check out
helpline numbers both in this chapter and on page 139.**

Kerryanne's advice

**I can understand the need for people to get out of the
house. It depends on what sort of problem you have;
I can only talk for those with my sort of family problem. I've been lucky because I've managed to get my
own place and I feel settled. I never felt safe when I
was away from home. It might seem like an adven-
ture at first but it's horrible not having a door you can
lock behind you at night. I was lucky too; some
people have to sleep on the streets. That must be the
pits – that night in the bus station was enough for me.**

**If your mum or dad has a problem, then Alateen is
brilliant because they will help you talk and find ways
to cope. It's a 'must do'.**

Contacts

Message Home Helpline
Tel: 0500 700740
A message can be taken and passed on to your family, for example if you'd just like to tell them you are safe. Please ring back if there is no one there to answer your call.

Shelter
88 Old Street, London EC1V 9HU
Tel: 0171 505 2162
Advice on accommodation for the homeless.

Young Minds
102–108 Clerkenwell Road, London EC1N 5SA

Write enclosing an s.a.e. for a leaflet advising young people whose parents may have a mental health problem.

Alateen
Al-Anon Family Groups (UK & Eire), 61 Great Dover Street, London SE1 4YF
Tel: 0171 403 0888
Send an s.a.e. for details of help groups in your area.

ChildLine
Tel: 0800 1111
Or write to FREEPOST 1111, London N1 0BR

Kidscape
152 Buckingham Palace Road, London SW1W 9TR
Tel: 0171 730 3300
Can help and advise if you have been threatened or abused by an adult.

"I'M PSYCHIC"

Photograph posed by model

"I'd always known that I had special psychic feelings, just like my dad and his mother before him"

15-year-old Sandra has been in touch with the spirit world ever since her brother died in a terrible accident. But having this sort of amazing gift has given her problems too ...

> **"We got a message from Richard to say that his death hadn't been traumatic"**

" **I'd always suspected that I had special psychic feelings, just like my dad and his mother before him, but it's not something that my dad wanted us to get into because he's quite scared of his abilities. Then my** brother Richard died in a sky-diving accident when I was 11 and that was very harrowing for us all. But that's when it all started to come together for me because my mum started to go to the spiritualist church and would sometimes take me along with her. We got a message from Richard through another medium to say that his death hadn't been traumatic and that he'd actually felt like he'd fallen from one world to the next. He said he hadn't been in any pain and we weren't to worry about him – that was such a comfort to us all. I got interested and then through the church, I was taught to improve the psychic skills I already had. Now I can get all sorts of messages for other people too.

I seem to have a talent for something called psychometry, which is when I pick up an object belonging to some-one and can read all sorts of information from it. A while ago the head medium did a little experiment at the church and she went round with a tray and asked some people to place something of theirs on it. To test me, she asked if I could hold something and tell everyone three things about the person it belonged to, though I hadn't seen who put what on the tray. She stopped me after I'd got 28 messages and most of the things were right. It can almost get like reading a good book. Once I'm really into it, it can be difficult to stop!

> "The man just couldn't believe what had happened, he thought it was amazing"

I do test myself sometimes too. There was one time my mum and I were on a train and Mum got talking to a businessman sitting opposite us. He was drinking a lot and so when my mum happened to tell him about my psychic abilities he said he wouldn't believe us until he had seen for himself. He got a gold locket from his briefcase and gave it to me. As soon as I held it in my hand I picked up a woman's name and also the image of a very old black car. When I told him he went very pale and told me that the name was of his last girlfriend. As for the old car, he said that this woman's father had died in a car that sounded very similar to the one I had described and the locket had originally belonged to him. The man just couldn't believe what had happened, he thought it was amazing. It really gives me a lot of satisfaction when I'm right about a message I have received. I have to accept that I get it wrong sometimes, but that can happen to the best mediums too. For a while, even though I was sure I had a gift I got a bit paranoid, thinking that maybe it was always just a fluke when I got the information right. Now I'm sure it must be more than that.

> "Some people at school are a bit wary about my abilities and get the creeps about them"

Some people at school are a bit wary about my abilities and get the creeps about them. We went on a school trip a while ago and one of the girls asked if I could regress her into a past life, because that's something I have learned to do too. I agreed after she bugged me about it for ages and took her into a room by herself, and I asked the others to be quiet because I didn't want her to be disturbed by their noise because she might get a headache. Of course, word spread around and people started to say that if she was woken up unexpectedly she could die or I wouldn't be able to bring her back. It was rubbish of course, she was fine. I got her back to her previous life at the start of the 20th century, I don't know exactly when. She said King George was on the throne and that her name was Ebony and told me lots of details about her family and where she lived. When she came back to her normal state she was the only one who didn't freak out about what had happened. She really enjoyed the experience.

There are all sorts of different areas to explore. I'm into reading auras at the moment because it doesn't take as much out of me. I was taught how to do it at the church. Everyone has auras all round them like a bubble. They can be physical, emotional, your desires, traumatic events, future, present and past. Everything about you can be discovered through the magnetic fields around your body. These appear in different colours and I have been taught to interpret them. When I learn something new I usually start by trying it out on some friends and so far I've had some great results. I can't see the auras, but I can sense them, so I have to slowly put my hand towards a person. When I get to a certain point before touching them I will feel what's like a tingling sensation on the palm of my hand and it's then that I will pick up information. If I sense they have a very green aura I'll know they are very calm, or I might sense a red spot around their leg, so I'll know that maybe they've broken it in the past. I haven't learned how to use the future aura yet so I can't tell friends things they don't already know, but it's fun for them to test me and see if I can tell them things about what's happened to them before.

> "I've stopped receiving and passing on messages for the time being because I've got more school work"

I don't feel bad that I've got this gift, mainly because I can block it out and stop it whenever I want to. I've stopped receiving and passing on messages for the time being because I've got more school work to concentrate on. I need to have my head clear most of the time and I've found that's impossible when it's cluttered with those sort of things. I've had messages from my brother to say that he thinks I should leave it for a couple of years because he wants me to have a more normal life.

I may not know what the future holds for me, but I do know I will go back to using my gift in later life. I might even study with other mediums to improve my skills, and make a tour of spiritualist churches, passing messages on to people. I don't ever want to lose the talents I've got but I want to keep them at bay for the time being. For example, when I go to college next year I am not going to tell people what I can do because I don't want more bad reactions. I never force my beliefs on others because it's up to the individual what they think is true. I don't have a problem with it – being psychic seems like such a normal part of my life now that I can't imagine why other people think it's a big deal. But all I can say is that those people who don't believe in the spirit world are in for a big shock when they get there themselves one day! People might think they are going to go into a hole in the ground and that's it, but I've seen so much proof that I know that's not going to happen ...

Could you be psychic?

Everyone has some sort of sixth sense, but how in touch with the paranormal are you? Put a tick beside the things you normally do and we'll check out your psychic ability.

☐ When the phone rings I can usually can guess who's calling.

☐ If thoughts of an old friend pop into my head for no reason then I'll usually bump into them over the course of the next few days.

☐ Sometimes I will write a word down and suddenly someone on TV or radio will say the word at exactly the same time.

☐ I look up to try to see a friend just a split second before they come into view.

☐ I say the same thing as my friends at exactly the same time.

☐ I get a worried, unsettled feeling for no reason and then find out later a loved one was in danger at that time.

☐ I hum a tune and then turn on the radio to find it's being played.

☐ I can guess exactly what a friend is thinking about when she goes quiet.

☐ I feel ill at ease in certain buildings without really knowing why.

☐ If I instinctively take an instant dislike to someone I'm usually proved right in the end.

Do you have the vibe?

Count the number of statements you ticked. Score one point for every tick you made and now we can tell you if you're in touch with the mysterious side of your personality.

If you scored ...

0–3
You should listen to your 'inner voice' more, although you probably think there's no such thing as psychic ability. Have a little faith and learn to trust your instincts more. You might be surprised at the insights you'll gain.

4–7
You have strange 'feelings' when things are going to happen and often put your spooky insights down to chance. Try our psychic exercises and you may be able to develop those skills further and *really* see into the future!

8–10
You are so sensitive to things going on around you that you feel as though nothing much comes as a surprise any more! You can read situations and people very well, so use your psychic insights to help make life easier – and avoid danger too!

Psychic exercises

- Draw seven symbols (e.g. star, circle, square, triangle, rectangle, diamond, oval) on different pieces of paper and ask a friend to choose one and concentrate on that shape for the next two minutes. When the time is up, stare at your friend, letting all the shapes run through your mind for a further two minutes. Guess what shape she chose, and if you get it right ... you may have 'the gift'!

- When you're in that 'in between' state between consciousness and sleep, try to think of yourself floating up from your body and looking down on the bed. Many people have trained themselves to have out-of-body experiences this way, and spend their nights flying through the air!

- If you suddenly have a very bad feeling about going somewhere or doing something, it might be best to trust your instincts. According to experts, women are best at predicting stressful events – even disasters! And after the seventh month of pregnancy, scientists have shown some women have an outstanding ability to see the future.

- Don't be afraid to pick up on 'vibes' you may have. You may not want to say anything if you feel like a friend is hiding the fact that she's upset, scared or angry. But ask her if she feels like you suspect she does, and she could be amazed – and maybe relieved – that you caught on to her true feelings.

- Learn a new word at random from the dictionary every day. If you have a 'gift', no matter how weird the word you have chosen is, you'll hear someone else use it in the next few days!

Sandra's advice

If you think you have some sort of psychic gift then don't panic about it, because it's normal. I'm sure everyone has ability but some people just don't want to use it. If you don't want to then you can always shut it out, like I do sometimes. If you feel like you want to use it then go to a spiritualist church and just ask them about it. But please tell your parents first and makes sure they know what's going on.

Other people might not understand or be willing to listen to what you have to say, and you have to respect that. Don't force your views on anyone.

One thing I wouldn't advise is confusing psychic games, such as trying to tune into friends' auras, with something more serious, such as ouija boards. They're not to be played around with and I would advise people to stay well away from them.

Contacts

The Spiritualist Church
Look in your local phone directory under 'Spiritualist Churches'. Visitors are welcome.

The Premonitions Bureau
BBC White City, 201 Wood Lane, London W12 7TS
Log your spooky dreams or premonitions with this office and they'll keep a record of your predictions for research purposes. Remember – this is a serious experiment, so please don't hoax!

"MUM AND DAD WOULD HATE THE BOY I LOVE"

Photograph posed by model

"They'd love me to go out with a nice English boy"

15-year-old Janine lives with her mum, dad and younger sister. She's fallen totally in love with her boyfriend, Al, but daren't tell her parents that she's met the love of her life. Al may be the right boy for her, but he's the wrong colour for her parents ...

66

Al is the first boy I have ever felt like this about. It's definitely love, but the only people who know about it are our very closest friends and they have been sworn to secrecy. If my mum and dad found out what was going on there would be *serious* hassle.

> "I have always known how racist my parents are and have been really embarrassed and annoyed by it"

I have always known how racist my parents are and have been really embarrassed and annoyed by it. My mum was up in arms when she found out there was a West Indian girl in my sister Laura's class. We were horrified when we found she brought up the subject of 'racial elements' at the next parents' night. My dad's the same. They're the sort of racists who think it's wrong when other people are bigoted, but they call black people 'darkies' and talk really slowly to anyone who isn't white because they assume they won't speak English. I don't get on particularly well with them anyway, but that does it for me. They're so ignorant.

I met Al at school, in my drama group. He is really funny and he wants to be an actor when he leaves next year. We've even talked about going to drama college in London together and getting a flat away from people like my parents. Al's mum is Ugandan, but from a Sikh Indian background, and his dad's family came over from India in the '60s. Al is quite distinctive looking, far too Asian for my parents to accept. They'd love me to go out with a nice English boy and are always asking 'what such a pretty girl is doing without a boyfriend'. It would be lovely to turn round and tell them I've met somebody really nice, but it's not worth World War III.

> "I said, 'Yes, he is Asian, actually, I do have eyes.' I hated her hypocritical attitude"

I see Al every night on the way home from school, but we're in a big group of friends who come home that way together. He lives in the estate near us, and when he splits off to go over that way my friends Sam and Louise walk with him. That's how I found out he fancied me in the first place – he confessed to them that he liked me and they put the word in. I was so chuffed because I thought he was gorgeous, but the first insult came from another girl in the group, Denise, who said, 'But he's a Paki.' This was the same girl who walked home every day with him. I said, 'Yes, he is Asian, actually, I do have eyes.' I hated her hypocritical attitude, like it was OK to be Al's mate, but not his girlfriend.

> "They were so friendly, it made me feel so ashamed of my own parents"

Louise sorted it out for us, and Al and I had our first date at the pictures, to see *True Romance*. Afterwards he took me to his cousin's restaurant and I met his mum and brother, who worked there. They were so friendly, it made me feel ashamed of my own parents. That's where Al and I had our first kiss and I was completely bowled over by him. He was very sensitive and interested in what I had to say. Everything I said made him laugh, and vice versa. When I got home it was nearly midnight and my dad was waiting up for me, demanding to know what was going on. I should have told the truth from the very start but I didn't want anything to spoil such a fantastic night and lied that I'd been at Sam's and we hadn't realized the time because we were watching a video.

When I saw Al at school he asked me out again and

suggested he call in for me and we could go for a walk. I was bit hesitant, and he picked up on it right away. I couldn't deny it when he asked if I had a problem with him coming round. He was so brilliant when I tried to explain what my parents were like. They didn't even like foreign food, never mind their daughter seeing an Asian lad.

Al did say that I would have to make my mind up what I wanted to tell them because it would be very difficult to have a hidden relationship. His parents let him see whoever he liked, but he still understood my problem. It didn't stop him going on at me to have it out with them but I was so mad about Al I felt that arguments and fights with my parents could mean the end of us two. I was hardly ever at home anyway – we spent every evening together, with me always saying I was at Louise's or Sam's or a new evening drama club I'd dreamt up. I didn't like lying, but it had to be done.

Then my sister Laura asked me one night if I had ever been out with an Indian bloke – she'd been hearing rumours. She really took me by surprise so I told her I had. She asked if Mum and Dad knew about it, and we talked about it for ages in her room. She thought I should tell them, because it didn't look like the relationship was a short-term thing. She came downstairs with me for a bit of support. I started off by saying, 'Dad ... what would you say if I came home with an Asian boy?' and he blanked me for a moment and then said, 'Why are you asking?' I told him I had been asked out by someone but if it would cause trouble I'd turn him down. My mum was listening in, and she said, 'Janine, the day you come home with a Paki is the day I die.' My dad laughed and said, 'Does that answer your question?' I was so upset and angry,

I went to my room and cried for ages because I hated them. It was such a horrible thing to feel the way I did about Al and not be able to tell everyone. Laura told me I should never tell them, and how could I after that sort of reaction?

> "We loved each other and that made all the bother with my parents seem insignificant"

The next night when Al and I met it was even more intense between us and I had to tell him everything that had been said, which was hard. He shook his head and said, 'They're sad.' But that night was the first time we said we loved each other and that made all the bother with my parents seem insignificant.

That was four months ago now and I still see Al – we're inseparable. There have been a couple of comments from people at school, saying 'Paki-lover' and stuff like that, but I just tell them to get in the 20th century. I don't know what I'll do if my mum and dad ever find out, but we'll think about that when it happens.

I hope one day we can have a place of our own so we don't have to worry about my parents. I'd like to leave home next year anyway, so we don't have too long to wait. I'll put all the photos I have of me and Al in frames and I won't have to hide them under my bed any more. If we get married one day I'll be able to invite my mum and dad to the wedding and then not care if they refuse to come or to acknowledge Al. I only wish it was as easy to ignore their opinions at the moment.

How would you handle it if they hated him?

It's natural to have arguments and disagreements with your parents about boyfriends, it's all part of growing up. But what's the best way to calm the waters? Try our quiz and find the best way to make peace with your mum and dad ...

1. Would you ever share the fact that you fancied a new boy on the scene with your parents?

a Yes, it would probably crop up in conversation at some point.

b No way – your parents are absolutely the last people you would tell.

c You might do, but only if you thought it would wind them up.

2. Word gets around and he eventually asks you out on a date. Where do you tell your parents you are going?

a On a hot date with a new boy – what else?

b Out with a couple of mates to do nothing special.

c To spend the night with someone they probably wouldn't like very much.

3. If your mum and dad were to ask what he was like, you'd probably tell them ...

a Every detail, right down to what his mum and dad do for a living.

b Everything you think they want to hear about him because that should keep the peace.

c Everything they don't want to hear about him so it annoys the hell out of them.

4. There's a big family party coming up soon. What do you think of maybe inviting your boyfriend?

a Great idea. It would give him the chance to meet everyone for the first time.

b Not a good idea, just in case he's not what they expected and it causes problems.

c Hmm, it would certainly cause a bit of a stir and give the relatives something to talk about.

5. The idea of leaving your boyfriend to chat with your parents makes you feel …

a Comfortable, because you're sure they'll get on without any problem.

b Worried that he lets slip you're seeing him when you say you're with your mates.

c Sure that this is one encounter that will lead to a massive family argument.

6. If your parents admitted to you that they really didn't like this boy how would you feel?

a Totally gutted, because you always thought you had really good taste. What do they know that you don't?

b Wary, because you know you won't be able to say you're still seeing him if they ask.

c Not in the least surprised. It's not often they approve of something you like.

7. And if they told you never to see him again, you would probably think …

a They must have a really good reason to dislike someone so strongly.

b That you'd better tell them he's as good as chucked but still see him behind their backs.

c That they were totally out of order and you'd better tell them that your boyfriends are none of their business.

8. If you two were to grow apart and split up through natural causes, you would feel ...

a Unsurprised, because your parents didn't think he was right for you anyway.

b Relieved in a way because all that 'double life' stuff can get really tricky.

c So disappointed that you couldn't make the relationship work and prove your parents wrong.

How did you score?

If you answered mostly a

You have an open and honest relationship with your family and can probably never imagine wanting to lie to your parents about something as important as a boy you like. It's easy – if you like him then they probably will too. Make sure you keep them involved in your love life without letting them interfere. You realize that the way to earn their trust is to show you're responsible, and so far you've been lucky. But what happens if you fall for someone far removed from your usual 'type'? Let's hope they're just as understanding then ...

If you answered mostly b

You have never thought boyfriends and parents are a good combination, and that's why you try to keep them as far apart as humanly possible. If they do ever meet, you and your boyfriend are going to have to pretend you've only just got together because he's been kept a secret for so long. Or worse still, someone else will tell them all about your blossoming love life before you have the chance to do it yourself.

If you answered mostly c
You almost get a kick out of seeing someone that you know your mum and dad are not going to approve of. Does that mean you go for objectionable lads, or is it more a case of your parents having very high standards? There must be some common ground somewhere, though, and one day you might realize how handy it is having a boyfriend that *everyone* likes. It might not be very exciting that way, but it means you could spend less time arguing with your parents and devoting more of it to having a great relationship!

Advice

If your parents hate your boyfriend

Talk to them
So they hate the idea of you seeing this boy. Rational conversation might not come into the equation when they're shouting, or when they just give a plain 'because we *don't*' when you ask why they don't like him. Inconvenient as it may be, your parents only want the best for you and if they don't think this boy is right for you then it'll take a lot to change their minds. There's no point in arguing and screaming to get your point across, although it's tempting! Try to have a reasoned, adult conversation to find out the reasons why they object to him and to see if you can change something about the relationship to make them approve of it.

Don't lie about where you're going

You can't tell your parents you're going out with him?
The natural temptation is to say you're seeing a mate
instead and start leading a double life, but these
things have a habit of getting complicated. If you're
found out then you're not going to be allowed to see
anyone – because you'll be grounded for a lifetime!
So if you do see him, try to meet in places you'd normally go anyway. Involve him when you and your
friends go out, or ask him to meet you from school or
work. Don't, whatever you do, sneak him into your
house when your parents aren't there. Nosy neighbours could get you into *big* trouble!

Let them meet him

This is only a good idea if your parents are quite
rational people. If there's any danger of a punch-up
then it's not advisable! They may think your boyfriend's not right for you, but if you know the truth to
be different then the only way to change their minds
is to let them see for themselves.

Find a mediator

Is there someone close to your parents who could
smooth things over for you? If you've tried to talk to
them with no results then perhaps a friend or relative
could put a word in.

Be truthful with your boyfriend

If your parents disapprove of your boyfriend, then it's
only fair that you should tell him. This can be embarrassing, because you'll have to admit that they are
racist or ignorant, or that he's just not up to their standards, but hopefully he'll understand that these things

don't run in the family. If you are going to remedy the situation then you are going to need his help too.

Don't see him to spite them

Some people think it's a bit of a thrill to deliberately see someone they know their parents won't approve of. So your mum hates blokes with earrings? You might, even subconsciously, be attracted to boys like that because you know she wouldn't approve and it makes things a bit more exciting. It can be fun to rebel, but you could be in for a real battle if you choose to see him. It's not fair to involve him, and not worth the extra effort you'll have to make, unless you're serious about him and the feeling is mutual.

Janine's advice

I can't tell anyone how to make their parents accept the 'wrong sort' of boyfriend, because I haven't been able to do that myself yet. The way I see it, you have each other and although you'd like to think nothing else matters, it doesn't always work out like that. I think you have to be very secure with your boyfriend to be able to risk a battle at home, because if the lad's going to chuck you in a few weeks it might not be worth the bother. One day I will tell my parents because it's got to come out eventually but I will only do it if I can leave home if things get bad and I can't do that till I'm 16 anyway.

If you are seeing someone your parents hate then I wish you a lot of luck. It can be hard because you might have to give up one relationship for the other, so think about it really carefully before having that confrontation.

Contacts

The Children's Society
Margery Street, London WC1X 0JL
Tel: 0171 837 4299
Work in England and Wales to help and advise young people and their families.

Children First
15 Annfield Place, Glasgow G31 2XE
Tel: 0141 552 3422
Work in Scotland to prevent abuse and problems in the home.

Youth Access
Tel: 01509 210420 (Monday to Thursday 9–5.30, Friday 9–4.30)
Provide information and counselling specially for young people.

OPUS (Organization for Parents Under Stress)
Endway House, The Endway, Hadleigh, Essex SS7 2AN
A wide network of groups providing support *for parents rather than children*. Pass the details on if you are giving your mum and dad hassle!

Anti-Racist Alliance
PO Box 150, London WC1X 9AT
Will provide information on how to deal with racism.

Asian Family Counselling Service
74 The Avenue, London W13 8LB
Send an s.a.e. for details of counselling service for inter-racial couples. At least one partner must be Asian.

"I WAS OBSESSED WITH A STAR"

Photograph posed by model

"I knew Stuart wasn't like any other boy I had ever liked"

When 18-year-old Rachel looks back on her idolization of a well-known pop star, she can't believe just how far she went to try to make him feel the same way too ...

It all started when I saw Stuart acting on television when I was about 15. If you could have put together all the things I found attractive in a boy then Stuart would have been that lad. I couldn't believe how cute he was and from that moment I made sure I saw everything he did on telly.

Then I heard he was a guest at a magazine road-show and I persuaded a mate from school to come along with me to see Stuart. He came on stage with

his co-starring actress and she started pulling his top up and stroking his chest to get a reaction from the crowd. Everyone went wild and I just burst into tears because I was so jealous and upset that she had the chance to be all over him. I think that's when I realized the depths of my feelings for Stuart and knew he wasn't like any other boy I had ever liked.

> "I couldn't stop thinking of him and my bedroom walls were plastered with pictures of his face"

I couldn't stop thinking about him, and my bedroom walls were plastered with pictures of his face. Then I lied to my school friends and told them that I'd started dating a lad called Stuart, but no one suspected I'd made it all up. They were always asking when they could meet him but I would say he was at work or he had flu and couldn't make it. I told them he was a DJ and had to travel a lot and that he was in his 20s, because I knew that would make them jealous. I did think they might catch me out one particular night when a mate had arranged a double date at the cinema. The three of us stood outside the cinema waiting for 'Stuart' to turn up although I knew he never would. I pretended to go off and phone and when I came back I made up a story that his car had broken down. That night I started to feel guilty and thought maybe the joke had gone a bit too far.

By then the 'real' Stuart had got a recording deal and I had the chance to see him far more often than I used to as he did a lot of promotional work. I'd made a whole set of friends because I always swapped addresses with other fans. We'd ring each other with news and dates of Stuart's next appearances.

176

> "I'd be outside the venue beforehand so I could see him arrive, and he'd say, 'Oh, it's you again'"

> "Once, I hid outside his room and actually saw him going along the corridor in just his Calvin Kleins"

If I wanted to see him I'd use the money from my part-time job in a newsagent's, or I used to ask my dad for money. I'd get some old, scruffy shoes out of the back of the cupboard and tell him I had to have some new ones. Then he'd give me £60–70 and I'd immediately book the train and organize a room in whatever hotel Stuart would be staying in. I'd be outside the venue beforehand so I could see him arrive, and he'd say, 'Oh, it's you again.' I was made up when he noticed me and stopped to chat, and some of the other girls would get jealous. Then back at the hotel I'd try to follow him. Once, I hid in the hallway and actually saw him going along the corridor to a mate's room in just his Calvin Kleins. He had the most amazing body, but although I wanted to shout out, I couldn't let him know I'd seen him. I wanted to be a friend, not a fan.

> "When his singles came out, I'd buy as many as fifty copies"

There was nothing I wouldn't have done for him. When his singles came out I'd ask for money again and sometimes buy as many as fifty copies. When I think about how much money I have spent on him it really must run to thousands of pounds.

My mum obviously knew I was obsessed but she didn't realize how far I'd go until I suggested that she needed a break and we should go to Spain for a week. I knew so much about him that I even found out where he was going on holiday, so when we arrived it wasn't long before we saw Stuart. He was there with Alison, a girl the papers said he was dating. When Mum found out he was there she was quite upset that I had suggested the holiday because of Stuart, not her.

When we got home I tried a bit of an image change, because now it was said he was very serious about Alison. I dyed my hair blonde like hers and if I saw her in a magazine I'd go out and buy clothes similar to what she'd been wearing. I once travelled about 300 miles because she'd mentioned she'd got these really unusual trousers in a certain area of London. I came home devastated because I couldn't find them in any of the shops. One day a friend saw Stuart at a gig, and when she asked about Alison he said they'd split up. They said in magazines he was totally cut up about it and although I felt relieved I was sad he'd been upset and resented her for hurting him. She was so lucky. Even if I'd had the chance to have slept with him just once then I would have been satisfied. I was gutted that nothing happened between me and Stuart, but then I suppose the good thing to have come out of it all was that I found my own boyfriend because of him.

Beforehand, other boys had asked me out and I would never have gone because I was too much in love with Stuart. But then, about a year ago, I met Christian in a nightclub. I was standing at the bar and when I looked up I thought I saw Stuart, he looked so much like him. I'd had a few drinks, so I went up and told him so. He said, 'You're not the first girl who's said that.' That was it – things just progressed from there, and when Christian and I hit it off I never felt the same way about Stuart again.

My love affair with Stuart finished for good one night after a gig when we were back at the hotel. I'd booked in alone and when I said hello he was really 'off' with me and I couldn't understand why. Then he invited about five other girls up to his room right there in front of me and I thought to myself, 'Forget it, he's just not worth the heartbreak.' He suddenly had a very bad attitude. I went straight back to my own room and cried my eyes out because I knew it was all over and we had never had the chance to be together. I didn't sleep all night, thinking how I had wasted so much time and effort on someone who was obviously not worth it. Next morning, I left the hotel as soon as it was light and that was the last time I ever saw Stuart.

I know it must be glamorous to have a famous boyfriend, with all the parties and photographers, but I know what I've got with Christian is the real thing. He's worth ten of someone like Stuart, even if he's not famous. I think now I am finally happy with what I've got.

Are you a Number One fan?

How far would you go to impress a star? Could it turn into a dangerous obsession – or are you unimpressed by the fame game? Try our quiz and find out if you really do worship your idol ...

1. You open a glossy magazine and see your hero showing off his new girlfriend. What do you think when you see her?

a What a slut. What has she done to deserve someone like him?

b She looks like a really nice girl and I hope they'll be very happy together.

c Don't her roots need touching up? And look at those shoes!

2. Your cousin reveals that he used to play football with your fave celeb before he was famous. What are you dying to ask him?

a If he knows where the star lives so you can sit out-side his house and wait for a glimpse.

b If he really is as nice a bloke as he looks on the telly.

c If he used to have smelly feet when he took off his football boots.

3. Mr Celeb is on camera at a star-studded party when he slips over and falls flat on his face. What's your reaction as you watch on the news?

a You burst into tears because you really hate to see your beloved make such a fool of himself in public.

b You feel sorry for him, but feel glad you've got it on tape, just the same.

c You burst out laughing because that should take him down a peg or two!

4. You've waited all year for your idol to appear in concert in your town. Where are you straight after the gig?

a Trying desperately to get a backstage pass before you head off for a night in the same hotel as him.

b Lugging the T-shirt, programme, baseball cap and tour jacket onto the bus home.

c Halfway home already because you left before the finale to beat the rush.

5. You're just leaving a restaurant when you spot him in a corner table, having a very serious discussion with a bloke who looks awfully important. What would you do in a situation like this?

a Rush over and ask the serious-looking bloke to take a photo of you and his famous pal snogging.

b Stare for a moment and feel like you're taking a mental picture to take home with you for ever. You've breathed the same air!

c Scuttle out because you don't want to be seen to ogle him. It's just not the done thing.

6. There's a competition on your favourite Saturday morning TV programme to win a date with your celeb. What do you do to make sure you win the prize of a lifetime?

a Send a letter written on loo roll with your entry post-card. It says "Please let me win" about 25,000 times.

b Cheat, but try not to make it obvious, by writing ten postcards in different handwriting.

c Send in one boring postcard and cross everything possible for luck.

7. The day he announces he's retiring from showbiz you are ...

a Locked in your bedroom crying your eyes out and wondering *why* ...

b Sad, but happy you had such a good time while he was in the limelight.

c Wondering how soon you'll be able to flog some of that merchandise you've got for a profit.

8. Rumours spread in the tabloids that your hero has been involved in a bit of a sex scandal. It's going to be all over the papers. What do you do?

a Refuse to believe what people say and send him a letter of undying support via his management.
b Read all the press reports, stay glued to the telly and debate the issue with your mates at every opportunity.
c Go off him totally and wonder what you ever saw in him. Pervert!

If you answered mostly a

There's a difference between admiring a celebrity and worshipping them. You have probably gone far beyond admiration and might even think you're in love with the star. You'll devour every little bit of information you can get your hands on, and no doubt you're screaming at the very front of those crowds at his personal appearances! Think about it – when you're more familiar with his public face than his private personality, can it really be him you love? Enjoy being a fan, but try not to let it rule your life.

If you answered mostly b

You love being a fan, but know that stars need their privacy too and would never be tempted to cross the line from simple interest to invasion of privacy. Go ahead and worship from afar because you are probably the sort of fan most celebs love to have. You'll buy the records, see the movies or watch the show, but you won't think that you have the right to own him just because he's famous. If you want to get in touch, join a fan club. You'll be slightly closer to your idol than the rest of the crowd, and that's certainly enough for you.

If you answered mostly c

It may be that you are a bit cynical, but the thought of actually falling in love with a famous person makes you want to laugh. You can't imagine ever wanting more than a bit of entertainment from a star and would far rather fancy a lad you have a chance of getting your hands on at some point! Fancying a star can be good fun, but you'd never take it seriously enough to feel bad if you never met him. You're too much in the real world for that.

Advice

If you fall in love with a famous person...

- Remember you have fallen for an image he's created, and you might not feel the same way about the real-life person. Not many stars are going to be horrible to their fans or come across as nasty in magazine or telly interviews!

(183)

- Don't shut yourself away from the possibility of relationships in the real world too. Rachel says she always felt that other lads who asked her out weren't good enough in comparison to the star she loved. You might not be lucky enough to meet a lookalike, so why not try a 'normal' date if you're asked? It may not be the most glamorous night of your life but it will be for real.

- Don't get upset if other people tease you about your obsession. They probably think it's funny to subject you to ridicule because they think there's no hope of you fulfilling your fantasies.

- Talk about your feelings if you think things are starting to get out of hand. If school work and friendships are suffering then it may be time to take a close look at the way you feel about your idol.

● Hard as it may seem, you shouldn't get upset over your celeb's own private relationships. If you really do admire them then you should be happy if they are happy – even if it's another girl who is making them feel that way!

● Believe it or not, you will probably go off him after a while, though right now it feels like you could be in love for ever. Just ask your mum what she thought of Mick Jagger and you'll see what we mean!

Rachel's advice

When you're obsessed with a famous person it can get to the stage when you think you will never get out of it, but you will, I know. When you love someone so much, all you see is the pop star or the film star and you don't see what they are like when they are at home or just living their ordinary lives. When you do see that side then you don't want to know because you realize just how normal and unexciting they are. I saw that side of Stuart that night in the hotel when his mood changed. He had such attitude and was acting too much like a normal bloke. I'll never be attracted to another famous person again because it's not worth it. You'll always be waiting, for the next gig, for the next magazine interview, for the next chance to see him. You have to ask yourself if he's really worth it, and I know that if he's anything like Stuart, he more than likely isn't.

Contacts

British Association for Counselling (BAC)
1 Regent Place, Rugby, Warwickshire, CV21 2PJ
Tel: 01788 578328
Publishes lists of counselling organizations and individual counsellors and psychotherapists throughout the UK.

Obsessive Action
PO Box 6097, London W2 1WZ
Write for info if you are worried about obsessive or compulsive behaviour.

Remember to send an s.a.e. for information.

"I'M SO ASHAMED OF MY SHOPLIFTING"

Photograph posed by model

"My parents would be mortified if they knew the sort of thing I've been up to lately"

Jackie is 15 and from Manchester. Her best mate introduced her to stealing and that resulted in a six-month shoplifting spree that left Jackie feeling guilty, ashamed and lucky to be without a criminal record ...

My parents have always brought me up to be honest and reliable and I know they would be absolutely mortified if they knew the sort of thing I've been up to lately, especially with my friend Emma because she can do no wrong in their eyes.

I go to rugby games every Saturday with my dad and little brother and we used to bump into a colleague of

my dad's. He said he was going to bring along his daughter next time because she was the same age as me, and I looked forward to seeing another girl in the crowd because I was the only one! When I met Emma at first I couldn't believe she was the same age as me. She was very tall and had lovely long blond hair – all the boys fancied her. At half-time we went down to the toilets together and I remember having a real laugh with her. We seemed to be hitting it off well because she had such a good sense of humour and we had loads in common.

> "I was shocked and quickly looked round to see if anyone had noticed her stealing"

I started to see a lot more of Emma than just at the rugby games and after a couple of weeks of knowing her, we decided to meet up to go Christmas shopping. As we went round the mall she made a comment about how expensive things were. She didn't have to tell me – I only got £2.50 a week pocket money and couldn't find any sort of Saturday job. Emma didn't work either so I didn't think twice about her moaning. But then, when we went into a big chemist, I saw her taking a tube of foundation and putting it straight in her pocket. I was shocked and quickly looked around to see if anyone had spotted her stealing, but we seemed to have gone unnoticed. When we got outside I couldn't believe what had happened but in some ways I got a bit of a buzz out of it, just like she said she had.

> "When I realized we had got away with it I got this massive buzz"

Before long we were meeting up every weekend and for a while I didn't lift anything, I just watched out for her. But gradually I started to take little things for myself, like lip balms and eyeshadows. Then once, we arranged to meet in town and my mum had given me money for a new skirt. I saw one that I really liked in a department store and Emma said to me, 'You don't want to bother paying for that, you know. It's not like there's an electronic security tag on it.' She told me to cover her for a minute, by standing where she told me to and she dumped it in her bag. I was absolutely petrified because we'd never stolen anything so big. I was sure we were going to get caught, but Emma was so cool about it. She said, 'Let's go and get some underwear to go with that', but I made some excuse because I felt sick with fear. But again, once we had got out of the shop and realized we had got away with it, I got this massive buzz.

> "I felt like I was, in effect, stealing from my own mum and dad"

My mum wanted to see what I had bought when I got home and when I tried the skirt on to let her see I felt a sudden surge of guilt that I still had the cash in my pocket. I felt like I was, in effect, stealing from my own mum and dad. They would have gone mad if they'd known I was going to spend all the money on cigarettes and going out with mates, but it also felt so good to have some spare cash on me for once.

I guess I was a bit scared of Emma. She was always overpowering and had to be the centre of attention all the time and I don't think, looking back, that I was a strong enough person to have been able to tell her that I thought she was going too far at times. I mean, one day we sat on the bus counting up the value of little things we'd stolen that day. We'd gone out without any money, but we had over £120 worth of stuff, just in our pockets. I didn't always feel good about what we had done, but that brief moment of enjoyment when we got away with it felt too good. She probably learned from her friends, the same way I was learning from her, because she was always talking about the things she had nicked with them. She boasted that they had once nicked a massive bottle of vodka from a supermarket and then gone and drunk it all – she even kept the bottle as a trophy to show people how daring she had been.

Then, one day, I was in town with Emma and she was thirsty, so decided to go and get a can of Coke from a big store in the High Street. Of course, we didn't pay. As I got a bit further down the street I got the shock of my life when this woman came up to us and asked if she could see the receipt for the drink. Emma was totally cool and explained she'd left it in the shop, so the lady asked if we would go back with her to sort things out. She showed us through the staff entrance and we ended up in a dark basement room under the shop. The manager came in and looked at us and I was so scared my legs were shaking and my stomach felt terrible. He said he was going to give us two options. Either we were going to tell our parents what we had been doing when we got home, and he'd be ringing to make sure we did, or he was going to get the police involved and see what they made of it all.

"What would happen if I got caught stealing clothes or expensive make-up?"

Of course, we both said we'd tell our parents, and I went straight home and told them what had happened. Who knows what Emma did. I told them I'd had the bad luck to be with someone else who had been stealing. I felt awful, with them thinking I was an innocent victim when they didn't realize that loads of the clothes, underwear and make-up in my room had never been paid for. They would have been devastated if they knew. As it was, they were really understanding about it and Dad phoned the shop to let them know I had told them. I decided there and then that it had to stop. I thought if they were going to act on one little can of drink, then what would happen if I got caught stealing clothes or expensive make-up?

Sometimes, now, I see things I like a lot and I know I don't have the money to buy them. I try to tell myself it's not worth the risk, and I hated that feeling of not being able to stop myself, and the guilt that the price of the goods I had taken could have been coming out of some shop assistant's wages.

I hardly ever see Emma now because she's got a part-time job and she's in the shop most nights. I really don't know if she's stealing from them too, but I doubt it – she's got enough to buy the things she likes now. My parents still think she's the greatest thing ever but they don't know Emma the way I do. We might keep in touch in the future but I can't see us being great friends in five years' time, say. She could have got me into a lot of trouble and that's not something I would expect from a true mate.

Are you an honest shopper?

Ask yourself the following scruples questions. Answer as honestly as possible, and we'll see if security guards should be on the lookout for *you*.

1. You see a shoplifter being followed by a security guard. In the chase that follows she drops her bag of goodies almost at your feet. What do you do?
a Take the bag back to the store and explain.
b Have a quick glance round before grabbing the swag and making off.

2. You know that the shop you are in has made record-breaking profits for the year. How does that make you feel when you shop in that store?
a No different. Shops are there to make money, so you'd never dream of stealing from them and reducing their profits.
b That surely they can afford to have the odd thing shoplifted, since they're so rich.

3. You see a rough-looking boy put a CD in his pocket in a record store. Do you tell the staff what you have seen?
a Yes, though you're a bit scared he might have spotted you telling on him.
b No way. That's grassing, and it's none of your business anyway.

4. You see an old man put a loaf of bread straight in his bag in a supermarket. Do you tell the staff what you have seen?

a Yes, but you feel bad about it because he might have been hungry.

b No way, it's not as though he's stealing expensive luxury items.

5. When you're selecting your sweets from the pick and mix counter, you …

a Usually give in to the temptation to test a few sweets as you go along.

b Wait until you've bought the goods before you sample them.

6. You're sure the girl beside you is about to nick something, but she hasn't seen the security guard just behind her. Do you warn her?

a No, but you stand around to have a nosy at her getting caught!

b Yes, and you hope someone else would do the same thing for you.

7. The girl at the till gives you the change from a ten pound note, even though you gave her a fiver. Do you tell her about the mistake?

a Yes, because she might lose her job if the till is short at the end of the day.

b No, because it was her mistake and you're skint!

8. You leave a shop in a hurry because you're late, but when you get home you realize you've shoved that mascara you were looking at in your pocket by mistake. It really is a genuine error, so what do you do?

a Go back to the shop and explain what's happened because you can't live with guilt!

b Give yourself a big pat on the back for getting away with it. What a result!

How did you score?

If you answered mostly a

You are either a trainee policewoman, or should be thinking about it! No need to follow you down those aisles, everything you want to buy goes straight to the checkout, not in your pocket. But don't let yourself be tempted! It might seem easy to pinch from shops and your mates might have got off scot-free so far, but it won't last. There are so many people with criminal records who regret stealing things they didn't really want in the first place. Make sure you are not one of them.

If you answered mostly b

You think shoplifting's a bit of fun, but have you made up your own mind about that? Don't follow friends who think it's just another leisure pursuit, because you'll be in trouble too when they get caught. And if you go out by yourself on 'shopping' sprees you'll get deeper and deeper into trouble. You'll have to explain where the goods come from to your family, you could be getting staff into trouble and you're not likely to get away with it for long. Take our tips and don't bow to the pressure ...

- You might feel pressurized to try stealing because everyone else is doing it and it does take a lot to say no. But why should you have to explain yourself to them? They only want you to join in because it makes them feel less guilty anyway.

- Real friends won't pressurize you to steal, so don't believe them when they say they think you should experience 'the buzz'.

- Don't turn a blind eye to your mate's shoplifting. Even if you don't get involved you could get hauled into the manager's office too if she gets caught, so stay at home if you know she's planning to shoplift this Saturday.

- Don't agree to act as a lookout. If your mate asks, tell her you don't want to help her get into trouble, and walk away.

- Don't agree to take her stolen goods home. Your parents might start to suspect you've taken them yourself!

- Think about how good your friends are for you if you feel uncomfortable in their company. You're not meant to feel threatened and frightened when you do something as innocent as going shopping with your mates.

Advice

If you are tempted to shoplift...

Remember: you're being watched!
A sneaky look around the store and it might seem to you that you're in the clear to tuck something in your bag or under your jacket. But you may not have spotted the video surveillance cameras, two-way mirrors and store detectives! Retailers know how shoplifters operate and if you are even considering stealing it might be more obvious to other people than you think.

You'll get caught in the end

You've probably heard stories going round school of people nicking the most outrageous things and getting away with it. Why shouldn't you have a go if it's so easy to get the stuff you want without having to pay for it? The simple answer is that you are extremely likely to get caught! It might seem like a bit of a giggle, but when someone asks to see your receipt the last thing you'll feel like doing is laughing, believe us. It's scary!

Shoplifters are breaking the law

You can try to justify your actions in all sorts of ways …

"High Street shops make too much money anyway."
Yes, and a proportion of that money is spent making sure people like you get caught!

"I only steal little things that don't cost much money anyway."
As far as the store manager is concerned, it doesn't matter what the stolen goods are. The rules apply to anyone caught stealing *anything*.

"I'm not a real criminal."
If you walk out a shop without paying, you are. And you could end up with a criminal record to prove it!

"Loads of people get away with it, why shouldn't I?"
Those mates are going to get caught at some point too; it just isn't their turn yet!

You could be fined or prosecuted

Another myth about shoplifting is that shop managers won't bother to prosecute if it's the first time you have been caught. Granted, as in the case of Caroline's friend, there may be occasions when the store manager might decide not to get the police involved. But they are very rare and there's no way you can tell what will happen when you take goods without paying.

Think before you do it
Whether the item you're stealing is valuable or not, the cost in terms of damage done to your reputation when you're caught could be far more. Is it worth it?

Jackie's advice

You have to find some strength of character if you feel pressurized to try stealing. When I got involved with Emma at first I would probably have gone with whatever she said because I wasn't always sure of myself. But I know now I should have made a stand, and if it all happened now then I would probably have ended up yelling at her when I spotted her taking that make-up.

197

If you are shoplifting at the moment then my advice would be to get out of it as soon as you can, because you really are going to get caught at some point. It's inevitable because store detectives always keep an eye out for teenagers and sometimes it can be so obvious when someone is taking things. When I look back I feel so ashamed and I feel like I let a lot of people down. There was so much pressure at home and school that it gave me something else to focus on, but that was the wrong sort of thing to spend my time on. If you are in the same situation, please stop before it's all too late and you get into serious trouble.

Contacts

The Children's Legal Centre
University of Essex, Wivenhoe Park, Colchester, Essex
CO4 3FQ
Advice line: 01206 873820 (2–5 p.m. every day of the
week, except Wednesdays 10 a.m. to 12 noon)
Advice on all legal matters concerning young people.

"I TRIED TO KILL MYSELF"

Photograph posed by model

"It would be better for me to go than to be so unhappy for the rest of my life"

15-year-old Rebecca can't say she has completely re-covered from the terrible depression that caused her to try to kill herself. She feels that her life is worthless, and that trying again may be her only option ...

Even when I was really young I used to get very depressed. I remember lying in bed when I was about 6 or 7, not wanting to get up to go to school because I didn't see the point in it all.

As I grew up I used to go through stages of terrible unhappiness and depression, and the silliest things would spark it off. If I didn't win at sports, if I didn't get the part I wanted in the school play, it all got me down and I'd be in a terrible black mood that would last for weeks and weeks. I would refuse to eat anything and I wouldn't care about how I looked or what I wore. No one ever talked to me at school because they said I was a weirdo.

I don't have brothers or sisters, but my parents never gave me the sort of attention usual for an only child. They have a distribution business which they run from home, so they never really switched off after the 9–5 the way some parents do. The phone would be ringing well into the night with orders and enquiries from clients; it was like an open house, but no one ever wanted to talk to me. I got very used to keeping myself amused because I didn't have many good school friends to bring home either. At weekends I used to spend most of my time listening to music and reading books while Mum and Dad coped with the business.

> "When I got home at night I just stared at my books and crawled into bed"

Last year, when I was 14, everything and everyone seemed to be getting at me. I would shut myself away in the loos at school and cry because I hated it so much. I couldn't cope with my work, and a teacher had told me that if I was going to do well in my GCSEs then I needed to pull myself together. She didn't realize that when I got home at night I just stared at my books and crawled into bed instead of tackling the stuff I couldn't get the hang of. Inside I was so tired and the easiest option was to shut it all out. I felt like it was pointless to try working because I would never understand anyway.

> ## "I used to tell my mum when I was feeling low, now I would just ignore her"

Things were bad at home too because the stress of work got to my parents and they spent a lot of the time fighting. My dad hit my mum a few times and I would sometimes sit in the park till 10 p.m. rather than face going back after school. I got more and more introverted, and whereas I used to tell my mum when I was feeling low, now I would ignore her.

It's hard to explain what you feel like when you contemplate suicide. It's not like something traumatic had happened to me that made me think I couldn't go on living. It was more a long process of realization that it would be better for me to go than be so unhappy for the rest of my life. I can only describe it as an escape from all the things I didn't want to have to handle. I was too mixed up to be able to explain myself to anyone, and I didn't feel like I wanted to talk. I thought I was the only person who could sort out my problems, and at the time that seemed like too much to cope with.

I bought a giant bottle of paracetamol from the chemist and looked in the bathroom cabinet to see what else I could take with them. I found some of my mum's sleeping tablets and took them too. Then I went into my room, put on a tape and swallowed everything with a bottle of cola. I was calm about it all, I didn't think about any of my problems, or anyone I wanted to say goodbye to, I just got in under the duvet and drifted off.

A while later I woke up and felt really bad. My stomach was cramping and I threw up all over my bed, but I felt so awful I just lay down again in the sick. I just remember someone pulling my arms and getting me on the floor beside my bed, onto my side. Then my mum trying to pour a drink down my throat and me being really, really sick again. They took me to hospital and I had my stomach pumped, which was awful, but I don't remember a lot about it, just that I was lying in the bed crying and crying but no one seemed to be speaking to me. Mum came with me and she didn't even ask why I'd done it, just kept going on about how everything would be all right now. I couldn't believe that it hadn't worked, but I was shocked because one of the nurses told me I was lucky I hadn't damaged myself permanently, because if I'd been found later my kidneys could have gone.

They kept me in till the next day and then I went home again, but my parents didn't discuss what had happened. The nearest we got to that was my dad asking if he should make an appointment at the doctor's for me, because I might want to talk to her about how I felt. I felt like screaming at him. My parents obviously didn't want to admit I had a big problem, when they had so many of their own.

I was sent back to school the next day like nothing had happened, and I have tried to pull myself together a bit since then and get into my school work again, but it's hard. I keep thinking of other ways to do it and next time I'll think about it more. I did go to see the school nurse to tell her I was depressed, but she was asking me if I was being bullied or had problems with a boyfriend. No one seems to understand that this is the way I have always been and it's going to take more than a little chat to sort my life out. If I manage to get any GCSEs I will try to go to a college to do a nannying qualification. I want to get my own flat and be my own person, but I'll have to get myself sorted first.

"I don't know how my family would feel if I'd succeeded in killing myself"

"There isn't much stopping me from trying again"

I don't know how my family would feel if I'd succeeded in killing myself. I suppose they would have blamed themselves for not realizing it was going to happen, but if they won't talk how could they hope to sort it out? I've only got a couple of friends at school, and they would hardly notice if I wasn't there because I've bunked school half the time anyway. There isn't much stopping me from trying again, but I sometimes wonder if things will get better for me if I make the effort. It's hard sometimes because I don't have the energy, but I might look into maybe talking to someone about it. I've got a few addresses of people who might be able to help and I might make a move on that soon, when I can face it. I don't know what the future will hold for me, but I hope I can face up to life for once, even though I know that might be harder than taking the easy suicide option.

Note: When MIZZ magazine interviewed Rebecca, we were able to give her some advice and contacts to help her with her problems. At the time of going to press she had spoken to her GP about her depression and was hoping to be referred to a counsellor to discuss her suicidal feelings.

Advice

If you are contemplating suicide

Let others know

Even if you feel like no one else could possibly hope to understand the sort of dilemmas you are facing, we can guarantee you are not the first person to have those problems. The first step to feeling better about yourself and the problems you face is to let someone else know how you feel. That could be a complete stranger (the Samaritans are there 24 hours a day) or someone who could help because they know you well. Please make that first step as soon as possible.

Is it fair?

The death of a loved one through suicide is the worst sort of grief for anyone to come to terms with. No matter how you feel about family and friends, please try to think how terrible it would be for them after you'd gone.

Time will help you

You feel as though you would like to end your life because you can't contemplate living your whole life feeling the way you do at the moment. But you never know what is just around the corner and things *will* get better for you in time if you get the help you need. Don't give up. You might not be feeling this way for long, so give yourself the chance to beat your problems once and for all.

And others can help too ...
Rebecca was very unlucky that she didn't receive any support from doctors at the hospital where she was taken, as many now have counsellors trained to help people treated after suicide attempts. Remember, it doesn't have to get to this stage before you can ask for help.

If a friend attempts suicide

Listen
Many people who reach such a level of depression may not want to talk to other people about their problems; but if they do, make sure you are there to listen to them.

Be aware of their problems
An unsuccessful attempt at suicide (parasuicide) is often described as a 'cry for help' and can be the person's way of alerting attention to their problems without actually telling anyone about them. When you do get to know about what's troubling them, keep an eye on the situation and offer as much help as you can.

Give them contacts
Pass on the names of people who can help and relevant agencies from our Contacts section.

Look for the signs
If someone has tried to kill themself once, they may try again. Keep watching your friend for danger signs and alert their family if you have to ...

Suicide: Can you recognize the danger signs?

You may be worried about a friend's situation, or the way their life is going. Tick the symptons you may have recognized already – some of them may be suicide warning signs ...

☐ Are they generally withdrawn or 'not themself' and acting out of character?

☐ Do they talk about suicide and even discuss ways of killing themself? (It's not true that those that talk about it rarely do it!)

☐ Are they giving belongings away, or generally clearing up areas of their lives they probably wouldn't want to leave behind in a mess?

☐ Are they unusually down and extremely sad?

☐ Do they seem to be in despair because they think there's no one out there who can help with their problems?

☐ Have they completely lost all self-esteem and think they are worthless?

☐ Have they stopped looking after themselves, perhaps forgetting to eat and wash?

☐ Do they seem to find it difficult to sleep?

Any of these signs could mean someone is feeling depressed or even suicidal, so if you have ticked one or more sections you must try to talk to your friend or get help for them as soon as possible. Support your friend, encourage them to keep talking and urge them to contact one of the agencies we've listed in the Contacts section.

If a friend commits suicide

Don't blame yourself
You can never know what went through that person's mind when they decided to end it all, so please don't blame yourself for not being a good enough friend to them and somehow being able to prevent their death.

Help their family

People might find it especially difficult to offer comfort to their family at this time because of the circumstances of the death. Explain that you are there if they need support, but it might be best not to offer your own theories when they ask the most natural question, "Why did it happen?" No one but the person who has died knows the answer to that question.

Grieve and remember
It's only natural for you to feel abandoned and hurt, even cheated, by the person who has killed themself. Try to concentrate on the life you had together and the good times you shared, rather than on the circumstances of their death.

Contacts

The Samaritans
Tel: 0345 909090
Wherever you are, you can ring the Samaritans on this number for the cost of a local call. They'll provide confidential emotional support for any crisis, 24 hours a day, every day of the year. They will listen without judgement for as long as you need to talk.

Youth Access
Tel: 01509 210420 (Monday to Thursday 9–5.30, Friday 9–4.30)
Provides information and counselling specially for young people.

Saneline
Tel: 0171 724 8000
Advice on mental health and depression.

ChildLine
Tel: 0800 1111
Please keep trying if line is engaged as they can get very busy.

"MY SO-CALLED MATE STOLE MY BOYFRIEND"

Photograph posed by model

"She just came out with it – 'Fran told me her and Jason can't keep their hands off each other.'"

Claire is 15 and lives in London. Until last year, she had a best friend and a boyfriend who got on brilliantly together. Now she has neither, and her whole future may have been messed up because of it ...

I was with Jason until last summer, and everyone always thought we were perfect together. He's really quiet and I'm quite loud and a laugh, so I brought him out of himself. I've seen him change a lot since I've known him, and not all the changes are for the better.

When we were younger, Fran and I used to laugh at

him and call him Spud because although he was quite nice he had a really fat face. Then he came back after the summer holidays when we were all about 13 and we were like, 'Who's that?' He had been in Australia for five weeks visiting family and looked different – tanned and he'd had his horrible long hair cut off. He was looking a lot slimmer and the joke going about was that he used to be Spud but now he was Stud!

"Fran never had a problem with me seeing him"

"I wasn't the jealous type at all. Not then, anyway"

I beat about four other girls to him – it was like a competition to see who could impress him the most. I knew I could make him laugh so I used to shout stupid comments and, I suppose, show off. Then I asked him out and that was that. Fran never had a problem with me seeing him. We live far apart anyway, so outside school we spent most of the time on the phone rather than meeting up. She didn't get jealous of us, and if she and Jason had lunch together when I was at swimming practice I thought it was good that they had become good friends. I wasn't the jealous type at all. Not then, anyway.

The only time I thought Fran fancied Jason was when I showed her some photos one weekend when she was staying over. I went to the loo and when I came back into the room she had taken a close-up picture of Jason out of the packet again to look at. It's not like they were just lying there, I'd put them away in my dressing table. I asked her what she was doing and she said she wanted to 'see them properly' or something. But she'd left all the others in the drawer. I don't know if she meant to take it, but I thought it was a bit odd, to say the least. That was the only hint I ever got. They were very good at hiding what was really happening.

We were all working really hard for our GCSEs – I was doing nine subjects because I want to do medicine eventually. It's really important to get good grades. Fran and Jason had eight, so we had lots of studying to do and didn't see a lot of each other because the mocks were coming up. Even though Jason and I were getting on really well I told him I was going to have to just see him at the weekends. I never wanted to split up – I thought we'd always be together. I didn't mind if he wanted to go out with his friends or if he wanted to study with Fran (they were doing History and German and I wasn't). I was sure everything would be fine when the exams were over. My mum had even said Jason could stay with us when his parents went to Portugal. I was even planning to sleep with him at some point soon.

> "Every time I tried to ask her if it was true my voice would crack"

The worst day of my life was the day I found out about them. There was this girl called Tina who we'd gone to Primary with, but who I hadn't really hung around with a lot. She was in a couple of my classes but nothing special to me, so when she turned up at my door I thought she must want to ask me something about our exam work. This was the week before our first GCSE in the summer, and we had time off school to study. She said she didn't want to come in but she had something she wanted to tell me for my own good. She just came out with it – 'Fran told me her and Jason can't keep their hands off each other.' I didn't have a clue at first, I was stunned, it's the only way I can describe it. I couldn't even react. Tina must have felt really bad, but she kept saying that none of the others had the bottle to tell me but she thought she'd better because there were a lot of people talking and I'd find out soon. I suppose she was only trying to help me but I slammed the door on her and sat on the stairs thinking I was going to explode. I felt like I was going to have a heart attack. I went all shaky but I picked up the phone and rang Fran, but her mum answered. She started to chat to me and ask how the studying was going and I lost it and started to cry. She was shouting for Fran and telling her there was something up, but when she came on the phone I was gasping and sobbing. Every time I tried to ask her if it was true my voice would crack, so I put it down. After ten minutes I knew it was true because she didn't phone me back. If there was nothing going on she wouldn't have been so scared to speak to me, and when I rang Jason to have it out with him the phone was engaged. I quickly called Fran and she was too. They were probably getting their stories together.

My GCSEs were a complete waste of time. I got mostly B and C grades, I couldn't study or remember anything I had already learned. I had to sit in the hall with both Jason and Fran for English, French, Maths and Geography – the four other worst days of my life!

I wrote Jason a note to say that I thought he could have had the decency to keep it a bit more discreet if he was going to cop off with my best mate and said a few things about him being too thick to have good taste in girls anyway. I didn't bother with Fran, she was beneath even writing to. I felt like I would probably have hit her if she'd come near me so I stayed at home for most of last summer, because then I couldn't see them together.

> "I don't want to hear the gossipy details from other people"

I could mess myself up more, thinking about how they got together and the lies they must have told. Maybe I gave Jason too much freedom. All I know is that I hate them both and I don't want to hear the gossipy details from other people. I have a skin complaint, psoriasis, which has come on because of the stress and my confidence has taken a complete fall. I will have to do my resits this year and hope this hasn't messed up all my ambitions too. Probably.

I will never forgive them, talk to them or even look at them if I can help it. They are beneath contempt and my only interest now is repairing my totally ruined reputation. Everyone knows what happened and they don't talk about it. They don't talk to Fran either, which gives me some satisfaction. But then she's got her new boyfriend to keep her busy. I am too angry to let them know I even care about what they did, but I still cry about it. They deserve each other – I hate them both.

Could you be a two-timer?

Imagine you were talking to a mate about your general attitudes to love and romance. Now, look at the following statements and tick those you can honestly imagine yourself saying ...

☐ If I'm going out with a boy it doesn't mean I can't fancy other people.

☐ A snog's just a snog – it doesn't mean a thing.

☐ I have usually split up with previous boyfriends because I have met someone else.

☐ I would hate my boyfriends to look at other girls the way I look at other blokes!

☐ Commitment is something for old, married couples.

☐ If a boy shows an interest in me then I like to give him some attention back!

☐ I don't find it easy to be 'just good friends' with lads.

☐ People have said in the past that I'm a bit of a flirt.

☐ If I found out that a boy fancied me he'd suddenly seem a lot more attractive than he did before.

☐ I'm far too young to be expected to stay with one partner.

If you ticked . . .

0–3
There's not much chance of you being the unfaithful type. Never mind marriage, when you even say you fancy a bloke that means you have eyes for him alone. Now the difficult part is trying to meet a boy that can show you the same sort of loyalty in return!

4–8
You think if you're dating one boy and happen to have a little snogette with someone else then what's the problem? It's nice to get the attention from more than one bloke from time to time, but when you meet the right boy for you that's when you'll think about being the reliable type.

9 or 10
As soon as someone pays you a compliment your head is turned. It might be that you wouldn't normally give them a second glance, but if the chance is there then you might give them the benefit of the doubt and go in for the kill anyway!

Or could he two-time you?

Think of the sort of relationship you would like to have with your ideal boy. Now tick the attributes you'd like him to have and we'll find out if the love of your life could be likely to play the field behind your back ...

☐ He'd find it really easy to get on with my friends.

☐ I'd love him to have the sort of looks most girls would drool over.

☐ I'm not interested in the sort of 'nice boy' my Granny would love me to bring home.

☐ Once you've hooked a lad it's easy enough to keep him in your clutches.

☐ I would prefer it if we both had our own social lives with our own separate sets of mates.

☐ I'd secretly love it if other girls were really jealous of me being his girlfriend.

☐ I like the sort of outgoing boys who give everyone a laugh and are the life and soul of the party.

☐ I'd understand if he flirted with other girls – that's what gorgeous boys do!

☐ I would expect him to tell me straight away if he fancied another girl.

☐ I'm sure I could tell a mile off if any boy was being unfaithful to me.

If you scored...

0-3
You are more likely to want to date the sort of boy you can keep well and truly under your thumb. One look at another girl and they could be paying the price. Happy henpecking!

4–8
If he does go off with someone else it's probably as much bad luck as your fault. There's not much you can do to keep blinkers on a boy, but if you'd be devastated if you split up, try telling him that. He may get the hint!

9 or 10
You are the most understanding girlfriend a boy could hope for, and even if you spot him snogging the face off another girl you'll still feel safe in the knowledge he's yours for keeps. Yeah, and then you'll wake up!!

Advice

Can you make love last?

The debate rages on. Is it really possible to make the boy you fancy stay faithful to you once you do get your mitts on him? If you've managed to snog a saint and it could be you've made the catch of the century then yes, but if you're like every other girl then you might need to take note of some of these tips ...

Communication
This is the most important part of any relationship. You have to talk to your boyfriend to make sure you're still right for each other, and hopefully problems won't be around for long because you'll talk them through.

Laughter
Don't take things too seriously! As those counsellors say, "Couples who laugh together stay together" – or if you don't want to be cheesy about it, who wants to go out with a whingy old moaner?

Freedom
You can't expect to spend all your free time together, although when you first start to go out together, sometimes 24 hours a day wouldn't be enough! As the relationship continues you'll both have to compromise and accept that you both need a bit of space to be yourself as well as just 'the boyfriend' or 'the bird'.

Trust
When you both have those nights out with your mates, you'll have to trust each other not to go off with anyone else. No one can hope to guarantee 100% loyalty from a partner, but really quizzing him about every girl he even spoke to or looked at is going to drive him away in the end.

Commitment

If you want to enjoy a more serious relationship, you may need to have a certain degree of commitment. We're not suggesting you demand to get engaged to keep him, but it wouldn't be out of order to have a serious chat about what you both expect of the relationship.

Experience
It's unlikely that any of the first few boys you go out with will be the love of your life, no matter how you feel at the moment. With every new love that comes along you'll get a bit more expert in dealing with boyfriends and you'll get to know more about what you want from love. That means when the perfect boyfriend for you comes along you'll grab him with both hands – and be more likely to keep a hold of him too!

Claire's advice

"

I'm not saying you have to suspect your boyfriend and your friend if they just get on well together, because most people would have the decency to stay loyal to you. If you are unlucky enough to hear rumours that something is going on then get proof first. Confront them if you can – I couldn't have gone through with that because I was too upset, but I knew anyway that the rumours were true by the way Fran reacted. Ask another friend who's prepared to tell you the truth. I could have talked to Tina for hours probably but it would have been even more upsetting knowing what Fran had said about my boyfriend. I really hope it doesn't happen to you. The two most important people in your life betraying you is not a nice experience. "

Contacts

ChildLine
Freepost 1111, London N1 0BR
Tel: 0800 1111
Phone free, or write to the postal address if you prefer (you don't need a stamp).

Tricia Kreitman
MIZZ Agony Aunt, 27th Floor, King's Reach Tower, Stamford Street, London SE1 9LS
Unfortunately, Tricia cannot enter into personal correspondence.

Family Planning Information Line
England: 0171 636 7866
Scotland: 0141 332 1216
Wales: 01222 342766
Northern Ireland: 01232 325488
Will offer advice and support on relationship matters too.

"I'M A 15-YEAR-OLD MUM"

Photograph posed by model

"I had a weird feeling I was pregnant. Maybe it was mother's intuition"

Terry, 15, lives at home in Bath with her mum and has a three-month-old baby boy. She had been together with her boyfriend for only four months when she got pregnant ...

When I was younger I always thought I knew how life would turn out for me. I thought I'd stay on at school for a while and then find some sort of job near to home and probably settle down in my early twenties. But then I was introduced to Liam by a mutual friend. His looks first attracted me, but when I got to know him I realized what a nice person he was. He made me

laugh a lot and it wasn't long before we were really close. Three months later I was pregnant and when I look back on it I can't believe how quickly things have happened to us. I didn't even expect the relationship to last, never mind us becoming parents together.

"I didn't get any sex education at school"

I didn't get any sex education at school. They only gave us information in one Biology lesson and I was off sick that day. As for chatting to my mum, we didn't have that sort of relationship. But even though I was still 14 at the time, I did make an effort to make sure I wouldn't get pregnant. I'd got it into my head that I didn't want to go on the Pill because I thought it would make me fat, but I made an appointment at the Family Planning Clinic soon after we started having sex to talk about alternatives.

"I felt like I had made sure I wouldn't get pregnant"

I was really nervous about going, but Liam said he would come with me for a bit of moral support and when we got there the staff were brilliant. We came back with free condoms and I felt like I had made sure I wouldn't get pregnant. Then one night we got carried away and didn't use protection. I knew that I could go to see my doctor to get Emergency Contraception afterwards, but I had already been along once for that already and thought he might get angry with me and give me a lecture if he saw me again for the same thing. I tried to get it from Liam's doctor, but he said that wouldn't be possible as he wasn't my GP.

I knew there was something wrong. I didn't have to wait for my period not to show. I had this weird feeling I was pregnant, maybe it was mother's intuition. Liam was worried about what had happened and bought me a testing kit, but I didn't get a proper reading. I decided to go back to the clinic, by myself this time.

I went along next morning, as soon as they opened, and after the test was done a nurse came into the consulting room and said to me in a very matter-of-fact way, 'Unfortunately you *are* pregnant. Would you like a termination?' I was upset at their attitude, to be honest. She could have been a bit more subtle about it and I sat there in shock, saying, 'I don't know what I'm going to do yet. I have to talk to my boyfriend and my mum.'

I walked out and went straight to school, explaining to them that I had slept in and was sorry I was late. I didn't know what to think about, sitting there in the class and I felt like it wasn't happening to me. Somehow, I wanted to tell everyone, but I knew that Liam had to be the first to know.

> "Liam and I both knew we couldn't go through with an abortion"

That night I went into the shop where Liam worked, on the way home from school. I waited until things were a bit quieter and said, 'You're going to be a dad.' He didn't say anything at first, but then he gave me a long hug and seemed happy about it. We'd already discussed it a bit, when he'd suspected I was pregnant and we both knew that we couldn't go through with an abortion. I think it's totally up to the individual, but I know it's never going to be the right choice for me.

I knew my mum had to be next, but I had to leave it for a couple of weeks because I had to pluck up the courage to talk to her – she could have prosecuted Liam because I was under age. I think she had some inclination there was something going on; after all she has had six children herself. So when, one morning, I asked if I could have the day off school because I wanted to talk to her the first thing she said to me was, 'Don't tell me. You're pregnant.' She didn't want to talk about it there and then because my sisters and brothers were around, but that night she took Liam and me out for something to eat, to talk to us about it. She said that what it came down to was this: if I was going to have the baby with Liam's support then she would stand by me, but if I wanted to get rid of it that was my choice. She was upset, but we'd made our minds up anyway. We were going to have a baby.

People at school were great about it and hardly anyone said they thought I was wrong to go ahead with the pregnancy. My tutor told the rest of the pupils when I wasn't there and from then on I had strangers coming up to ask if they could feel my stomach! There was one dinner lady, though, who said I was stupid for having a baby at 15 and I should have waited. I didn't think it was any of her business. Then my headmaster suggested I should go to a school for teen mums, near where I live. I was lucky I had that option and it's brilliant there – I get lots of support.

"When our son was born it was unbelievable and I cried the first time I saw him"

There were ups and downs throughout the pregnancy, and at 23 weeks I was rushed into hospital with forced labour, which means I was getting contractions too early. I was so frightened, especially when they gave me an injection to mature the baby's lungs to give him a chance of survival if he was born. It didn't come to that, though, and I was home again in a couple of days. From then on I took things easy, and eventually I went into labour exactly when they said I was due. Liam was with me every minute, and both our mums were there for the birth. I did have a lot of pain at first but I was given an anaesthetic so I spent practically the rest of the remaining five hours watching TV! When our son was born it was unbelievable and I cried the first time I saw him. What they say about the love you feel for your own child really is true; it's like nothing I'd ever known before.

Liam and I are engaged now and we've got a flat. We've done it up a bit and I'm going to move in on my 16th birthday. I can't think of one thing that I hate about being a mother. There are things I've had to give up, and I don't see my friends as often as I used to. Liam and I also get on each other's nerves a little bit more than usual, but that's because we both want what we think is best for the baby. But more than ever I am looking forward to being together, the three of us as a family.

Could you be a teenage mother?

Are you in danger of getting pregnant? See how much you know about the risk of unwanted pregnancy with our checklist quiz. Answer true or false to the following statements and keep a note of your answers.

1. You have the ability to get pregnant every single day of the year.
2. You have to have started your periods to be able to get pregnant.
3. Most teenage mums used contraception that didn't work properly.
4. If you have a hot bath straight after sex there's no danger of getting pregnant.
5. Most girls aren't actually able to have babies until they're in their twenties.
6. If you're under 16 a doctor will tell your parents if you ask him or her for the Pill.
7. It's possible to get pregnant without having full sex.
8. The Pill is 100% guaranteed to protect you from pregnancy.
9. There are certain positions you can have sex in which mean you won't get pregnant.
10. If the boy withdraws from you before he ejaculates you can still get pregnant.

Answers

1. FALSE

There are certain days in every woman's monthly cycle when she is extremely unlikely to get pregnant. The problem is, it can be very difficult (and decidedly risky) to guess when these days are. There are complicated ways of telling, usually involving taking your temperature and examining vaginal discharge. But who has the time? Isn't it far simpler to make sure that if you are ready to have sex, you are protected every time?

2. TRUE

When you start to have your periods your body is starting to produce the eggs which are your part of the baby-making process – when one of these eggs is fertilized by a boy's sperm a human life starts. Your period is your body's way of shedding those microscopic eggs and the womb lining that won't be needed this month, because you haven't got pregnant. That's why the first sign of pregnancy is a missed period: it's not going to happen because the egg has been used.

3. FALSE

Although a tiny percentage of girls may get pregnant because of split condoms or ineffective Pills, many teen mums would admit they just 'didn't think it would happen to me'. It's so easy to get swept along in the excitement and passion of sex that sometimes protection is only something you'll think about when it's too late or nearly too late. Try to think ahead, but if you do find you've gone ahead without protection, remember that the so-called 'Morning-After Pill' (real name: Emergency Contraceptive Pill) can be taken up to 72 hours after sex. Please ring your GP or clinic if you need further advice.

4. FALSE
No amount of water is going to wash away a pregnancy, so forget hot baths, showers or vaginal douches.

5. FALSE
As we've already said, from the moment you have your first period you are capable of becoming a mum. Your fertile period will usually last until your mid forties or early fifties, when the menopause means your periods stop and you are no longer capable of conceiving.

6. FALSE

Most GPs now agree that everything you discuss with them will be kept confidential, no matter if you are under age. That should also apply if the doctor is a friend of the family, or if one of your parents demands to know what's going on! If you feel unsure about the situation with your own family doctor, you can ask at reception if appointments for under-16s are confidential.

7. TRUE
It is possible to get pregnant without having penetrative sex. It is very rare, because because sperm tend not to live outside the warm, damp conditions of the vagina. However, if a boy has sperm on his fingers and puts them inside you, or if ejaculates (comes) very near to the entrance of your vagina, then it is possible to get pregnant in that way.

8. FALSE
Even if you take the Pill according to instructions, probably one in a thousand girls will have the bad fortune to get pregnant while taking it. Most people get pregnant when on the Pill for one of the following reasons: they've been sick or taken antibiotics, they've forgotten a Pill or taken it later than they should have done, or they've had diarrhoea. If in any doubt about the Pill's effectiveness, refer to the pack instructions or better still, always use condoms too.

9. FALSE
Sperm want to reach their target and nothing's going to stop them – apart from good contraception. That means they'll swim round corners if it means they hit the target and make a baby, so no sex position is going to stop them getting where they want to go.

229

10. TRUE
Even before the boy ejaculates (comes) sperm can escape from the tip of his penis, so even if he does practise the withdrawal method he might already be too late! Anyway, this is a really risky way to protect yourself because boys admit that when they're about to come, 'pulling out' feels like the last thing they would like to do.

How did you score?
Unless you got a full ten out of ten score, you are at risk. Please don't take a chance when it comes to risking unwanted pregnancy. It's so easy to get protection – all you have to do is phone a clinic or a GP for a confidential appointment; alternatively you'll find condoms at the chemist or in vending machines in pubs and restaurants.

Advice

Think you might be pregnant?

Warning signs include:
- Missed periods
- Swollen or tender breasts
- Morning sickness
- Peeing more often than normal
- Change in appetite

What should you do now?

Find out for sure

There are various easy ways of finding out for sure if you are pregnant. Don't put it off, because this might be a false alarm and then you will have worried over nothing. If you are pregnant, it's best to find out as soon as possible because then you'll have more time to discuss what to do. For example, if you decide that abortion is your best option an earlier operation is far safer for you.

Get a test done

GP, Brook or Family Planning Centres provide the service free. You'll be given a bottle or dish and asked to visit the loo to provide a urine sample. Some tests let the doctor know straight away if you are pregnant, but in other clinics you will be asked to come back in a couple of days for the result.

   Pharmacists often provide the service for a small charge. Take in a small sample of urine (you might want to use a clean medicine or lotion bottle) and come back later for the result.

Home tests are now quite reliable if you follow the instructions to the letter, but they can be quite expensive (£8–11). They're on self-service shelves in bigger chemists, such as Boots.

What to do if you are pregnant
In all cases, if the test isn't done by your doctor or a clinic and turns out to be positive, please make an appointment with either of them to discuss your pregnancy *as soon as possible.* Trying to forget about a pregnancy won't make it go away

Who can help?
It's not always possible to speak to your parents because they might not stop shouting long enough to have a sensible conversation! There are trained advisers at clinics like Brook and Family Planning Clinics, or you may want to ask for the help of social services to help sort your family situation out. Walk into reception at your nearest office and ask to speak to a social worker.

What are your options?

Keeping the baby
Choosing to go ahead with motherhood can be exhausting, if rewarding. You should be able to delay your school work, or the council may be able to arrange for you to have a tutor at home. If you are under 16 you will not be able to receive any benefit from the State, but ask at your local DSS office for more details of your entitlement.

Abortion
Two doctors must agree to refer you for an abortion

and there may be a waiting list if you opt for a free NHS operation. This can only be performed up to 24 weeks (although doctors rarely agree to the op at this late stage) so it's important to act as quickly as possible if you think this may be the right option for you.

Adoption
The child may be taken to a foster mother after the birth, but you will be given further time to consider if this is the right option for you before the adoption becomes legal.

Temporary fostering
Ask your Social Services Department if this is a possibility. The baby will be taken to a foster mother for an agreed amount of time – usually until you have found your feet after the birth or are more financially secure – then you will be given the baby back. Social Services will still take an interest in your welfare and try to help with the practicalities of bringing up the baby.

Terry's advice

Things have worked out all right for me, but you might not be so lucky. I'd advise anyone thinking about having sex to get down to the clinic, because they're really nice and will give you the advice you need. I'd advise you to use condoms, but go on the Pill too, to be extra-safe. If you do get pregnant then make sure you tell your boyfriend and your mum as soon as you can. It's never going to be easy, but it might not be as hard as you would have thought. They might surprise you with the support they give you.

Contacts

Family Planning Information Service
England: 0171 837 5432
Scotland: 0141 332 1216
Wales: 01222 342766
Northern Ireland: 01232 325488
For advice and support on matters concerning family planning, relationships, and sexual health, call your nearest info line.

Brook Advisory Centres
Tel: 0171 713 9000 (for details of your nearest centre)
Tel: 0171 617 8000 (for computerized helpline service)

Life
Advice Hotline: 01926 311511 (9 a.m. to 9 p.m.)
Can help teen mums with practical support (clothes, equipment, accommodation, etc.) and give advice on benefits and financial matters; although they can't, unfortunately, provide financial support.